EVALUATING MORAL DEVELOPMENT

and

Evaluating Educational Programs
That Have A Value Dimension

edited by:

Lisa Kuhmerker

Marcia Mentkowski

and

V. Lois Erickson

Character Research Press
207 State Street
Schenectady, New York 12305

International Standard Book Number 0-915744-24-4 (hard cover)
International Standard Book Number 0-915744-21-X (paper back)
Library of Congress Catalog Card No. L.C. 80-68348
First Printing

Cover Design
by
Robert Olbrycht

Typesetting
by
Helen C. Cernik

TABLE OF CONTENTS

Page

iii

Program evaluation and the measurement of student growth is a significant component of every educational enterprise. As a rule, books, monographs and articles focus on educational theory and practice and devote only a small portion of the publication to issues of evaluation. This is true for the literature in moral development and education as well. Each year hundreds of books and articles describe research and intervention studies, but none of them have been devoted exclusively to evaluation of moral development or programs with a value dimension.

The program planners of the 1979 conference of the Association for Moral Education were responsive to the desire of many members to have a meeting devoted primarily to the "state of the art" in evaluation. Several reasons made 1979 a particularly auspicious time for such a program:

> The last five years had seen the creation of several moral education projects at the elementary school, high school and college level and researchers and practitioners wanted insight into the process of evaluation in these projects;

> Lawrence Kohlberg and his colleagues at the Center for Moral Education had just completed a twenty-year study clarifying and validating the measurement of moral reasoning;

> James Rest was on the verge of publishing the results of almost ten years of work on his Defining Issues Test;

> Several new instruments were at various stages of development and field testing and there was need for an opportunity to "line them up" for comparison purposes;

> There was a growing awareness that specialists in moral education had to find ways to make their findings intelligible to teachers, administrators and parents if they hoped to get school and community support for the integration of moral development programs into the curriculum of the public schools.

The program of the 1979 AME conference was so timely and stimulating that it seemed appropriate to share it with a broader audience. We think of this as a book whose time has come, a book that will stimulate research and practice in the evaluation of moral development and education to such an extent that a book with a similar focus three, four or five years from now will make this volume look like a preface!

The membership of the Association for Moral Education and the conference presenters vary widely in their professional affiliations but tend to share some common assumptions which should be clarified for the reader at this point. If pressed to define our philosophical and psychological orientation, most of us would call ourselves cognitive-developmentalists. That is, we think of human beings as actively structuring and restructuring their concepts, their ideas of rights and responsibilities, their ideas of what is and what ought to be. We do not think of children as "tabula rasa," passively shaped by an environment on which they learn to model themselves. Life experience and social interaction are necessary for moral development. A certain amount of conflict or "cognitive dissonance" and reflection on the perspective of others also seem to be related to moral growth. We think of moral judgment as a prerequisite to moral—in contrast to merely social— behavior. We do not believe that all preferences, attitudes and values are moral values, but we believe that part of any process of value clarification is the capacity to distinguish between moral and non-moral issues, and that developing sensitivity to moral issues is part of the task of education.

Some of us were attracted to Lawrence Kohlberg's theory because it was based on this cognitive-developmental foundation. Some of us first saw structure in meaning-making when we looked at moral development through his theoretical lens. In either case, Kohlberg has been teacher, gad-fly, but above all, mentor, to most of the contributos to this volume. His work is well known to us, and he was not a "Presenter" at this AME conference, but readers can find an overview and synopsis of his theory and methodology at the beginning of the section on "Alternative Modes for Assessing Moral Judgment."

Kohlberg realized early in his career that valid and reliable assessment of moral reasoning was a critical concern for theory and research. In order to investigate moral reasoning and to clarify its place as an educational goal, it had to be pulled out of other aspects of development and education to become a subject for theory and research. Kohlberg and his colleagues worked twenty years to find a reliable and valid way to trace the sequential stage development of moral reasoning but this does not mean that we assume that the assessment of moral judgment is the only, or primary, goal of evaluation of programs with a value dimension. As we integrate moral development into the goals and procedures of the total learning milieu, we must expand our evaluation strategies to encompass a wide variety of outcomes that result from an integrated curriculum. This volume reflects a variety of initial efforts in that direction.

We begin with a setting forth of some perspectives and directions for evaluating moral development and program evaluation. James Rest describes and contrasts the models of development that have influenced theory and practice during the past ten years and highlights questions to which the evaluator of programs in moral education must be responsive. Marcus Lieberman points toward new directions in evaluation and illustrates their application to the evaluation of a Holocaust Curriculum developed for the eighth grade social studies curriculum of students in the Brookline, Massachusetts schools. Marcia Mentkowski stresses the need for creating a mindset for evaluation with examples from the outcome-centered liberal arts curriculum of Alverno College in Milwaukee, Wisconsin, which both teaches and assesses the "valuing ability" of its students. Also with college-aged students, but outside the academic curriculum, John Whiteley describes how the Sierra Project in Irvine, California created and evaluated a "Just Community." Each of these chapters illustrates the need to design evaluation models to fit particular programs and settings.

With this broad view of program evaluation and some elaborated examples as a beginning, we turn to a description of specific instruments and techniques that have been developed to assess moral reasoning and that insure some generalizability of evaluation findings from a broad range of program evaluation studies. We urge readers to think of these instruments and evaluation strategies as progress reports on the "state of the art," not as recipes in a cookbook from which to select a sample that might serve to satisfy the evaluation component of a project. Of all the instruments presented, only Kohlberg's Moral Judgment Instrument and James Rest's Defining Issues Test have been extensively validated. The other instruments are in various stages of development and field testing. We encourage you to take the time to become acquainted with the advantages and limits of each instrument, remembering that good programs have multiple goals and that evaluation strategies must seek to tap many kinds of growth and skill development in addition to the capacity for moral reasoning. We have included an Appendix with the name and address of a contact person for each instrument.

In the past, the complexity of the Moral Judgment Instrument has kept researchers from adopting it as a measure before having a clear idea of its applicability, but James Rest has horror stories to tell about researchers who asked for copies of the Defining Issues Test because it seemed like a quick and easy way to satisfy a doctoral committee or funding agency. This led him to a policy that is a true service to researchers: Rest asks each potential user of the Defining Issues Test to send him an abstract of the research proposal and if the DIT is suitable for evaluating the project, Rest sends not only a copy of the instrument without charge, but encloses scoring guides and an updated reference packet. As a result of this policy Rest has a unique resource file of hundreds of studies, some that have been completed and some that are still in progress.

The section on "Alternative Modes for Assessing Moral Judment" begins with Lisa Kuhmerker's detailed description of Lawrence Kohlberg's Moral Judgment Instrument and scoring procedures. Then in a dialog with Kuhmerker, Kohlberg gives us a glimpse into the history of his sequential stage theory, some of his current thinking on its use and place in the evaluation of moral education, and previews forthcoming data from the longitudinal study that validates his instrument. Then John Gibbs, Keith Widaman and Anne Colby describe a new measure called the Socio-Moral Reflection Measure, based on the Moral Judgment Instrument but opening up the possibility of a more easily scorable production-type instrument. Next, James Rest reviews the Defining Issues Test, the most widely used measure of moral judgment, in the context of research findings developed through the use of his instrument. James Carroll and Edward Nelsen discuss some of the problems encountered in the effort to develop an instrument for measuring the moral development of pre-adolescents. The next two chapters describe efforts to extend the principle of James Rest's Defining Issues Test to the creation of instruments that integrate the evaluation of both content and growth in moral reasoning in a single measure. Louis Iozzi and June Paradise-Maul underscore the importance of moral issues in the study of science and technology and suggest that this curriculum can be evaluated with the help of Iozzi's Environmental Issues Test. James Bode and Roger Page describe their development of the Ethical Reasoning Inventory, which they have used to assess the effect of an ethics course.

The section on "Alternative Modes for Assessing Moral Judgment" closes with two descriptions of more global evaluation strategies. V. Lois Erickson provides us with a progress report focused on case studies from her five-year follow-up study of a group of students originally enrolled in a high school developmental education course. Clark Power introduces us to the wide variety of strategies and instruments that are designed to provide insight into the moral atmosphere of the school. There may come a day when paper and pencil tests will provide an acceptable measure of long-term growth but if such a time comes, however, it will be because instruments using rating scales or recognition tasks will have been built on the foundation of understanding exterpolated from production-type instruments. We see this process in the sequential development of the instruments described in this volume. The Socio-Moral Reflection Measure is based on the painstaking analysis of countless protocols of the MJI. The DIT's recognition tasks are based on the stage theory that emerged from the MJI. The Environmental Issues Test parallels the DIT. The Ethical Reasoning Inventory seeks to combine the best features of the MJI and the DIT. When Clark Power began to interview students about the moral atmosphere of the school he was breaking new ground, so like Kohlberg with his early moral judgment interviews, he had to begin with a production-type instrument and detailed long-term observations.

Following the presentation of instruments and evaluation strategies we return to the issues of integrating moral education into the curriculum of the schools. Alan Lockwood assumes the perspective of a hypothetical group of school board members who are responsible for deciding which programs should be implemented, expanded or dropped. Edwin Fenton provides apt examples from his wide experience in the schools in general, and in civic education programs specifically, of the way in which moral education programs develop not only moral reasoning skills, but the very skills that traditional education seeks to promulgate. For a capstone we turn to Ralph Mosher who provides a fitting coda by outlining and qualifying the accomplishments of theory and practice in moral education during the last ten years. In the light of these accomplishments he calls on us to direct our efforts to the adaptation, integration and mainstreaming of moral education into the curriculum of the schools.

In translating a set of conference presentations into a balanced volume on the "state of the art" in the evaluation of moral development and programs with a value dimension, we have tried to preserve the combination of caution and confidence that characterized the proceedings. There was intellectual ferment, a willingness to assume the self-discipline that data collection and analysis requires, and—above all—a commitment to education in a democratic society. In this spirit the members of the Association for Moral Education and the editors of this volume invite you to share with us your ideas, your critiques and your colleagueship.

Lisa Kuhmerker
Marcia Mentkowski
V. Lois Erickson

Chapter 1

BASIC ISSUES IN EVALUATING MORAL EDUCATION PROGRAMS

James R. Rest

I'd like to characterize where we've been and where we're going in moral education with special attention to the role of program evaluation. We would define "program evaluation" in a rather broad way. We would include any activity which gathers information about an educational program on a large number of questions:

Did the program produce desirable changes in the students and were these changes enduring?

Are the psychological or sociological assumptions in the program rationale warranted when tested in the naturalistic "field" situation?

Which parts of the program worked best for which students?

What are the initial characteristics of students who profit most from the program?

What activities are actually going on, as opposed to what activities are supposed to be going on?

For which students were the optimum conditions for learning actually provided and how did these students do in comparison to others?

What is the teacher doing and what difference does it make?

What teacher characteristics and activities are most related to student development?

Are there some component skills which seem to be prerequisites for general development?

What difference do various curriculum materials make on immediate interest as well as long term effects?

How costly in terms of time and money are the various program components and what are the cost-benefit relationships?

How do earlier classroom activities influence and affect later classroom activities?

What influence do experiences outside the classroom have on experiences inside the classroom?

These and related questions are the many *specific* concerns of program evaluation. The *general* concern of program evaluation is to gather information about an educational program in action so that we can determine how worthwhile it is and moreover get information to help us improve the program the next time that we run it. Most evaluation to date has been focused on the first issue, on the big pay-off question, "Did the program produce desirable effects?" However, in the next 10 years I think the viability and momentum of the moral education enterprise is going to depend most on how we handle the second issue—namely, how can we get systematic information from programs as they operate which will put us in a better position to make them better in successive cycles of program development.

About 10 years ago in Toronto, Canada, a conference was held to explore what the Canadian Public School System might do in the area of moral and value education. Clearly the most exciting event of the conference was Larry Kohlberg's presentation of a cognitive developmental approach to moral education. I need not describe here Kohlberg's vision of what moral education might be. Although Kohlberg spoke of these ideas as "warmed over Dewey" mixed with some American extensions of Piaget, nevertheless these ideas provided the main philosophical rationale for a kind of moral education and a major psychological model for conceptualizing the processes of moral education. These two elements—the philosophical rationale and the psychological model of development—have been the chief attractions of the cognitive developmental approach. Ten years ago there were virtually no curriculum materials developed, no teacher training programs, and hardly any evidence that cognitive developmental programs were effective. It was the philosophical and psychological backgrounding that attracted people to this approach. Over the past 10 years much attention has been given to the development of curriculum materials, specification of teacher roles, teacher training, and there have been dozens of studies to determine if moral judgment was significantly enhanced by educational intervention. Don Cochrane's bibliography each year in the *Moral Education Forum* indicates the explosion in publications in this area; each year something on the order of 35 books and 200 articles are published. And so starting with Larry Kohlberg's vision ten years ago, a considerable amount of activity and progress has been made. What is crucial, it seems to me, for the next ten years is that ways be devised to collect information on the workings of these educational programs so that we learn something more about what moral development is and how it can be facilitated. In short, we've got a start; but to keep going we've got to develop a reciprocating process of doing programs, learning from them, developing new programs based on this information, and doing them again. I think in the next 10 years, new ideas about how to get useful information from programs will be as important as pedagogical ideas about program development.

In the past 10 years, evaluation has been of secondary interest and importance. Evaluation was something you had to do in order to get the money for the grant, or evaluation was necessary to get past your dissertation committee. The real interest was in program development—in developing ways and materials for teaching. And so with 5% of your grant budget, you'd bring in someone to fling a pre and post test at your students; or if you had no grant budget, you'd take a couple of measures off the shelf and grind out the scores. Many of us got grants and dissertations that way. What was more important, however, was the program idea. But if we are to move beyond our present stage of knowledge and programming, I think evaluation is going to have to play a major role, interacting with new ideas for program development.

I'd like to suggest some general trends in moral education and to cite their implications for evaluation research. Historically there have been two major theories of moral education, the Durkheim tradition and the Piagetian tradition. Durkheim portrays moral education in terms of changing the *motives* of the person. For Durkheim, moral education changes the motives of the student from selfish, impulsive, and unsocialized motives to having altruistic, disciplined, and socialized ones. The individual is "socialized" through direct instruction, example, and group reinforcement to acquire and accept the behaviors and attitudes that are constructive for the group as a whole and that conform to the norms of the larger society. On the other hand, we have Piaget (and Kohlberg, prior to perhaps 1977). Piaget's 1932 book is as much a statement of educational ideology in direct opposition to Durkheim as it is a purely "scientific" description of children's thinking. For Piaget, moral education ought not to be focused on changing people's motives in order to make them conformists, but rather ought to be focused on developing people's understanding of the possibilities and conditions of cooperation. Piaget and other cognitive developmentalists assume that as a person realizes what the possibilities and conditions of cooperation are, then the person will also feel a stake and commitment to actualizing cooperative social arrangements. They assume that as a person develops a larger picture of how he or she can relate to other people, the person's decision-making will be made from this larger perspective rather than from a more limited, egocentric, short-sighted one. With education, the person is liberated from ignorance, egocentrism, and prejudice; understanding leads to social responsibility.

These two approaches to moral education have traditionally been opposed to each other: the Durkheim/"socialization" school being accused of promoting mindless conformists and making the world safe for Fascists; the Piagetian/cognitivist school being accused of pie-in-the-sky unrealism, and making the world safe for nobody. In academic circles, the battle lines have also been drawn between the social learning researchers versus the cognitive-developmentalists. The social learning researchers have studied the impact of modeling and reinforcement upon marble-dropping behavior and coming to the aid of a tape recorder in distress. The cognitive developmentalists spent a decade figuring out how many different ways Heinz could justify stealing the drugs.

Now as long as these two theories of moral education and moral development were kept separate, the job of evaluating moral education programs seemed to be relatively straightforward. If you bought into the cognitive developmental orientation, then you pre- and post-tested the students on a measure of moral judgment and looked for the curriculum's ability to produce lively discussions with plenty of controversy, disequilibrium, and mutual challenging. If you bought into the "socialization" view, you looked not at thinking but at behavior and affect; you looked for solidarity and conformity, not controversy and disequilibrium.

Several things have happened to complicate the situation—for educational theory, for developmental theory, for program developers and for program evaluators. Kohlberg before 1977 was the most outstanding spokesman for a purely Piagetian point of view. But more lately, Kohlberg has advocated taking Durkheim more seriously. Hearing Kohlberg espouse Durkheim is a little disconcerting to some of us who have bought into the cognitive developmental theory, advocated cognitive developmental programs, fought against Brand X, paid our dues, and learned the cognitive developmental handshake. For some of us, hearing Kohlberg advocate Durkheim presents an emotional experience something like this: You are the First mate on a ship, taking your turn of duty at the wheel; you have been alerted that your course is about to take you into stormy seas, and then you hear that the captain of the ship has just jumped ship and is headed on another boat in the opposite direction.

I say this is the "emotional experience." I will come back in a minute to examine if this is the reality of this situation. But in any case, as Larry Kohlberg has reflected on the experience of actually developing and running moral education programs, he has introduced more variables and conditions which don't come straight out of classical cognitive developmental theory. Other program developers have shifted as well from regarding changes in moral judgment scores as the only outcome variable of importance, and from regarding the discussion of controversial moral dilemmas as the sole educational activity. For instance, Clive Beck and Ed Sullivan of the Ontario Institute for the Study of Education, which has the oldest moral educational program going, have shown these shifts to other program emphases and other outcomes variables. And so practical experience in the moral education business has led many program developers away from classical cognitive developmental theory. This presents an interesting challenge to the educational theorist. It leaves program evaluation in utter confusion.

Another, but related development, is taking place in academic research in moral development. The social learning theorists are getting more interested in situational and performance influences on moral behavior. Cognitive developmentalists have usually admitted that their stage models were "logical competence models" rather than complete performance models of how humans really function in actual situations; yet, only recently have cognitive developmentalists begun to study how moral judgment relates to actual real life behavior. The research literature is fairly consistent in showing that there is a moderate relation between moral judgment and real life behavior. But it also shows that moral judgment is not the *only* variable influencing behavior. Other variables also play a significant role, and they interact and mediate and complicate the relationship between moral judgement and behavior.

The research literature is so huge on other factors besides moral judgment which influence moral behavior that I cannot summarize it here but can only give some illustrative examples of these kinds of factors.

1. William Damon (1977) found that other values besides moral values can influence behavior. Damon asked children to describe a fair way to distribute candy bars. He found that what children said would be fair deviated from what they actually did. The pressure of their own self interest distorted their espoused plan of distribution. Other values besides moral values entered into the actual decision making.

Similarly John Dean in his book, **Blind Ambition**, recounts that his nefarious activities as special Counsel to President Nixon were motivated by unquestioned loyalty to that administration and by his own ambitions within it. Dean says that he constantly put aside the larger questions of morality— such questions were completely preempted by more pressing values.

2. Krebs and Kohlberg reported a study (in Kohlberg, 1969), of the interaction of moral judgment and "ego strength." Differences in "ego strength" are involved when two people have the same understanding of a situation and the same plan of action, but one has iron will, courage, and resolve, whereas the other person falters, is overwhelmed by distraction and pressures, and fails to carry through. Krebs and Kohlberg found that Stage 4 subjects with low ego strength cheat more than Stage 4 subjects with high ego strength—the subjects with low ego strength were less able to carry out their beliefs than those with high ego strength.

3. One of the most striking findings coming from research on bystander reactions to emergencies is that people fail to help others. But the reason they fail to help is not because of general apathy or evil intent but because of confusion (see Staub, 1979). In emergencies, people are often unable to define and appraise the situation or determine what, if any, personal action is called for.

4. Carol Gilligan's research (1977) has indicated individual differences in moral sensitivity. Some people seem to notice a

moral dilemma almost immediately with minimal cues, whereas others recognize a moral issue only after the most blatant signs of human suffering. If a person is morally insensitive, then no matter how sophisticated one's concepts of fairness, those concepts will not even be brought into play, much less determine behavior.

5. A considerable amount of research indicates that behavior is not always under the control of conscious, deliberated thought such as is revealed in moral judgment tests. For instance Piaget himself (1932) distinguishes different "planes of mental life": at one level, a "conscious-reflective" and articulated plane, at another level an "operative" plane consisting of non-vocalized, unreflective mental processes. A person's behavior can be governed at either level, but if one's behavior is governed by unreflective operative processes, then there need be little connection between what a person says on a moral judgment test and what he does in some instance of behavior. Typically, for children and perhaps for many adults, their behavior is largely reflexive, pushed and controlled by whatever stimuli and pressures happen to occur in the situation, little governed by some ongoing deliberated plan or consciously chosen set of decisions. Psychological research is as yet very incomplete on how behavior comes to be governed on the conscious-reflective plane, how a person's considered beliefs and plans and ideology come to be the chief determining force in one's life.

These examples of factors that influence moral behavior do not exhaust the list, however they give an impression of the kinds of things that complicate the relation of moral judgment with behavior. Psychological research is just beginning to investigate how these factors interact with moral judgment.

What's happening then in both the experience of program developers and in academic research is the growing recognition that many factors besides moral judgment are involved in moral development. This shouldn't be construed as a matter of "jumping ship" or completely disavowing all that has gone before; but it's a recognition that there are many players in the arena of human behavior; that moral judgment is just one of these performers; it may be a star performer, but it's not the whole show. In short, the facts of experience are making eclectics out of all of us. Now in general, I don't like eclecticism—eclecticism has always seemed to me cowardly and dull, usually disappointing, and only excusable in a freshman psychology course. Nevertheless the facts of the matter have forced our hand, and we seem to be stuck with a lot of variables, all interacting in complex ways. If it's true that neither Durkheim's nor Piaget's theory is complete, then we need a more comprehensive theory of moral education in order to settle on a comprehensive plan for evaluating moral education programs. Lacking all three, I will make some preliminary suggestions in that direction.

First of all, I think we have to regard Piaget's theory, the cognitive theory of moral education, as portraying an *ideal* situation of moral development. It is not a description of inevitable psychological processes. Understanding the possibilities and conditions of cooperation *can* lead to social commitment—but a lot of things have to go right for this to occur. These processes are unlikely to be very strongly consolidated in young children and many adults because their behavior is not under the governance of abstract ideology or long-term planning. So in the meantime, some system of social control is necessary to start them off in constructive directions, to prevent them from doing harm to themselves and to others, and to make it possible for social institutions to function. The long term goal of moral education does not obviate the necessity of shaping behavior before its rationale can be appreciated. In other words, there are occasions when it is necessary to use group pressure and exert authority.

Therefore a two-track educational approach seems sensible. One track would be designed to develop the incipient moral philosopher in people, to focus on the development of moral judgment, anticipating the time when the person will have formulated a critical moral ideology and appreciates his or her stake in making society work. The other track would be designed to shape behavior—as non-coersively as possible—so as to equip the child with socially useful skills and routines which he or she may not yet appreciate. Socialization is intended to prevent or limit destructive behavior, and to provide the experience of working in groups for shared goals. The influences of social example, didactic instruction and reinforcement would be employed to "socialize" the child, before moral rationality is developed or has much potency. Socializing comes before rationality is ready to take over. The "socialization" of the child must not be undertaken with such a heavy hand however that it stifles the child's critical powers and interest in seeking the rationale behind rules. Furthermore, the child should not be shielded from controversy or exposure to other points of view. In fact, I would advocate beginning programs that stimulate moral reasoning in the earlier years of schooling. The purpose of these activities would be to begin laying the cognitive groundwork that leads to progressively more adequate moral reasoning. No immediate payoff in behavior would necessarily be expected from the stimulation of cognitive development. Vandalism in schools and cheating on tests may not be affected by cognitive moral education at first. Cognitive moral education is a future investment in preparing people to function as envisioned in the democratic ideal.

Undeniably there is a tension between the two approaches: in particular, over the locus of control. The socialization approach vests power in the socializer and the cognitive approach delegates decision making to the child. Just as in parenting, the teacher will have no easy time in deciding how much power to give to the child. Yet unavoidably the child starts off with no power, but eventually the child must become the decision-maker. Transferring power from socializer to child is difficult, but essential in developing active participants in a democratic society.

Primary schools must begin the development of understanding about the structures of social cooperation, and also furnish basic information about our social institutions and the psychology of getting along with other people. However not until college is it likely that principled moral thinking (Stages 5 and 6) will mean something to many people. Principled moral thinking is quite abstract and requires imagining different ways of organizing society. Research to date indicates that the college years are most crucial in moving most people beyond conventional moral thinking. Furthermore, in the college years the control of behavior by ideology and deliberate reflective planning is likely to increase. In the years beyond high school the individual begins to see many choices, and begins to see the need to have a programmatic basis for making these choices. Although each developmental stage is crucial, it is during the post-high school years that the most substantial shifts to principled moral thinking are likely to take place and the greatest shifts to behavior governed by reflective, conscious planning.

The ultimate goal of moral education is to produce people who can reason in philosophically adequate ways; who can formulate plans of action even when under stress, or experiencing conflicting values and situational pressures; and who will actually follow through behaviorally on such plans. This ideal can fail at many points: a person may not be able to reason at higher stages, or may not be sensitive to the fact that there is a *moral* problem, or may be swamped by other pressing values, or just may not be able to follow through for reasons that involve personality and ego strength. Therefore, we need to be concerned about each of these aspects in moral education. Evaluation of programs should be concerned not only with moral judgment but also with moral sensitivity, moral character and moral values. While not diminishing the importance of the structure of moral reasoning, we also need to develop ways of measuring these other variables which also affect or determine moral behavior. Derek Bok has written a provocative article on moral education (1976) in which he says that "formal education will rarely improve the character of a scoundrel." However, he goes on to say, moral education might have impact in three ways: (a) "help students become more alert in discovering the moral issues that arise in their own lives" (this is essentially what I've called "moral sensitivity"); (b) "teach students to reason carefully about ethical issues" (this is essentially what I've referred to as "moral judgment"); and (c) "help students clarify their moral aspirations" (this essentially relates to the priority given to moral values over other values).

If we take this more complex view of moral development (as being more than just moral judgment) then an evaluation of moral education programs will want to look at multiple outcome variables. This means coming up with ways of measuring these other variables. If we want answers to the questions about educational processes that I raised at the beginning, then indeed we, the evaluators, have a lot of work to do.

REFERENCES

Bok, D. "Can Ethics be Taught?" *Change Magazine*, October, 1976, 26-30.

Damon, W. The Social World of the Child. San Francisco: Jossey-Bass, 1977.

Gilligan, C. "In a Different Voice: Women's Conceptions of the Self and of Morality." *Harvard Educational Review*, 1977, 47 (4), 481-517.

Kohlberg, L. "Stage and Sequence: The Cognitive-Developmental Approach to Socialization." In D. Goslin (Ed.), Handbook of Socialization Theory and Research. Chicago: Rand McNally, 1969, 347-480.

Piaget, J. The Moral Judgment of the Child. (M. Gabain, trans.) New York: The Free Press, 1965, (Originally published, 1932.)

Staub, E. Positive Social Behavior and Morality. New York: Academic Press, 1978.

Chapter 2

NEW DIRECTIONS IN EVALUATING
MORAL EDUCATION PROGRAMS

Marcus Lieberman

The title of this paper reflects three major issues which have attracted the attention of large numbers of educators, administrators and researchers. Evaluation has become a field in itself, with specific methodological tools, experimental designs and concerns for program implementation highlighting the recent activities of professional evaluators. Moral judgment continues to be investigated by psychological researchers and the domain of this construct is becoming sharply defined as we learn more about adult development, life crises and the moral reasoning of women. Education, to those interested in cognitive development, means more than information passed from one individual to another. By redefining education to mean development of reasoning ability, we open a whole new chapter in the area of classroom discussion or experience techniques. Challenge, conflict, resolution and growth represent a radical change from the way most people think of teaching and learning. I would like to address each of these issues separately and close with an optimistic view of the future.

EVALUATION

The focus on the outcomes of evaluation in the late 1960's produced several texts, guides and handbooks on how to specify, in measurable terms, the objectives of our curricula or units. In the frenzy of generating thousands of behavioral objectives, we elevated such men as Popham (1969) and Mager (1962) to a position of such importance that the preachers of this movement caused many of us to lose our perspectives on the educational processes themselves. In the Seventies we see this enthusiasm channeled into a more rational endeavor, that of a concern that the tests we use correspond to the goals of our teaching. Educational Testing Service, Harcourt, Brace Jovanovich and other giant testing companies must have shuddered slightly as test users became more articulate about just what these general standardized tests were and wern't doing for them. There has been some change in this industry resulting in criterion-referenced tests which are intended to measure specific strengths and weaknesses in various content areas, thus providing feedback to teachers in a way that percentiles and grade-equivalent scores could not. Unfortunately, all programs funded by state or federal funds must still show sufficient growth on a standardized achievement test before any results from other instruments will be considered. The specific topic of instruments used in evaluating moral education will be dealt with later.

The emphasis on outcomes was reduced slightly with the introduction of implementation or process evaluation. As program directors and administrators demanded information which was useful from evaluators, data about the nature of the instructional program including specific classroom processes and their correspondence to program objectives was sought. Program developers not only described the outcomes of their units, but also described the nature of the process that was expected to help the children attain them. Upon close inspection, however, Murphy's Law often prevailed in the following form: The degree to which a program looks the way an author intended varies inversely with the geographic distance between them. One Harvard thesis by Mayer (1973) showed more variation in program processes in sites within models of Headstart Programs than between different models! If program directors wished to claim that it was their program that caused changes in their students, documentation of classroom activities and the quality of discussions is essential evidence. This documentation usually takes the form of data gathered by the use of an observation schedule or rating scale. Literally hundreds of these process instruments have been published for a wide variety of educational settings and many appear in a multi-volumed reference by Simon (1970), **Mirrors for Behavior**. Extremely few, however, exist for constructivist or developmental education programs, although several existing instruments contain categories of student or teacher behaviors that proponents of such programs would like to see happening in their classrooms.

A second step back from outcomes involves the seldom considered area of program antecedents. A proper evaluation should include a discussion of the rationale for the program, documentation of administrative support, adequate training for the teachers and prerequisite skills for the students, appropriate time, materials, physical facilities and layout of the classroom. Then, if the program is improperly or inadequately implemented, it may be possible to trace the causes to one of those areas.

These three dimensions of project evaluation; antecedants, processes and outcomes, constitute the most recent notions of what quality evaluation should include. Activities related to these areas form a distinct departure from typical research activities where the efforts are toward adding to a knowledge base rather than providing information useful to a decision maker.

A second departure from traditional research appears in the context of experimental design. Rarely is the educational practitioner in the position of being able to randomly assign students to treatment or control groups, since classroom assignments are usually determined in a central office. The concept of quasi-experimentation, first introduced by Campbell and Stanley (1963), is most recently treated in an entire volume devoted to relevant issues by Cook and Campbell (1979). The limits of causal inference with non-equivalent treatment groups, statistical analysis of data and experimental validity are all discussed in a comprehensible manner.

A final area included in evaluation concerns statistical

treatment of data. While traditional tests are appropriate for continuous, normally distributed variables, the outcomes of moral education are likely to be qualitative rather than quantitative and require, more often than not, some non-parametric form of data analysis. It is unfortunate that most of us learned about the binomial and multinomial tests in the context of black and red balls drawn from urns rather than in any real situation. The recent appearance of several texts on the subject of non-parametric statistics, E. G. Siegel (1956) and Marascuilo and McSweeney (1977), is a direct response to the needs of researchers and evaluators whose data are not likely to conform to the assumptions of the traditional tests.

These then are some of the general trends in evaluation that apply in most educational contexts, though the implications for the field of moral education still remain to be sharpened.

MORAL JUDGMENT

Over the last ten years we have seen a change in the definition of moral reasoning. Kohlberg, his colleagues and other researchers in the field have provided us with a much clearer picture of several aspects of this psychological process.

Within Kohlberg's research group, the procedure for scoring responses to hypothetical dilemmas changed its focus from a content analysis approach to a structural one. Rather than focusing on the content concerns a subject used in resolving a moral dilemma, the emphasis shifted to the broader socio-moral perspective in which these concerns are imbedded. An early form of a scoring manual was produced which described this procedure. However, a combination of problems (e.g., the focus on ultimate justification or philosophic rationale being necessary for discriminating among the higher stages and the need for improved reliability among scorers) necessitated a further revision of this manual.

The Standard Form scoring technique defined a new unit of analysis, the Criterion Judgment. This constituted the smallest piece of discourse that could be accurately scored and is represented by the intersection of dilemma, issue, norm and element, all operationally defined in the latest version of the Kohlberg manual.

There is some discussion at the Center for Moral Education at Harvard about the narrowness of the domain of moral judgment defined by these criterion judgments. Some research in progress being carried out by Carol Gilligan and her colleagues suggests that moral judgments made by many adults and especially women confronting a divorce or abortion decision are simply not represented in the manual. She believes that, up to now, scorers have found rough matches in the manual for these judgments at the lower stages implying that women often are not found to be reasoning as high as men. Since a large proportion of the Criterion Judgments in the manual are drawn from responses of Kohlberg's longitudinal sample of males, she expects that examples of women's principled thinking would increase the validity of the measurement.

A second variable related to moral education is derived from Kohlberg, Scharf, Reimer and Power's works in defining the concept of the moral atmosphere of prisons, kibbutzim and schools, e.g., Power and Reimer (1978). The interviews developed in this research could be employed to measure either processes or outcomes. Students respond to a questionnaire designed to elicit their perceptions of the existence and nature of group norms as well as the phase of development of community consciousness. Thus it is possible either to monitor the evolution of a Just Community as seen by those involved as well as changes in the perceptions of the students about an existing environment.

A third variable to be considered as a potential outcome for a program of moral education is the ability to discriminate among moral judgments at a variety of levels. The Defining Issues Test or DIT developed by James Rest has been used widely for this prupose, and has strong evidence for its validity and reliability.

Finally, there is an area related to moral reasoning that is included in some moral education curricula. This area can be divided into two major parts. The first deals with cognitive skills that might be considered prerequisite to carrying on a discussion based on conflict in a moral dilemma. These might include developing an awareness of the existence of a conflict, articulation of both positions in a conflict, supporting the side with which you are in agreement, etc. These represent both affective and cognitive traits that, while often desirable, fall outside the specific domain defined by Kohlberg's six stages.

The second part is a blend of cognition and affect and is concerned with values clarification. Many moral education programs have as their goal to aid students in recognizing their own values, developing a consistent system of values and committing themselves to those things which they prize most highly. While there is no single instrument to measure these things, Raths, Harmin and Simon (1966) and colleagues give several suggestions for evaluating the effects of such a program. Rather than viewing Simon's techniques as an alternative to Kohlberg's model of moral education, they are best seen as complementary. A recent review of Simon's and Kohlberg's works by Colby (1975) described value clarification as helping people to know and accept themselves, to be able to choose freely and carefully. On the other hand, moral development strategies help people to test those values and choices with a moral perspective, and it is hoped, to act morally as well as sincerely.

EDUCATION

Kohlberg and Mayer (1972) described the aim of education as progression through a sequence of developmental stages. Using the works of Piaget and Dewey, they argued for an alternative to the naturalistic and information transmission models of education. Kuhn (1979) recently reviewed several applications of Piaget's theory to education. She advocates the need to define the competencies characteristic of a stage so that their application in a wide variety of situations would be clear. A second need is that of defining the nature of self-directed intellectual activity and the process by which it becomes developmentally transformed. She concludes with a plea for educators and developmental psychologists to work together to provide a comprehensive framework for constructive education.

Some informal collaborations of people like these have brought forth the beginnings of what this form of education might look like. Rather than totally centering on the child for the source of experience, or "teaching" him to mimic the reasoning of a stage higher than his present reasoning, they offer an interactive alternative. Present the children (or adults) with information which jars their equilibrium about social or physical phenomena. If the setting has been designed to be supportive and non-threatening, the opportunity for no-risk exploration in ideas and opinions is enhanced and children may begin to ask about the nature of knowledge itself, what Nathan Isaacs (1974) called the "epistemic question." By using a form of Socratic dialogue, the teacher and students can resolve some of these questions and perhaps cause the students to reason in a more complex way, taking more perspectives into account or applying reasoning used in a separate instance to the problem at hand.

The implications are numerous. Teachers must find or design materials or experiences which run counter to the child's expectations. The closer the phenomena to the child's own interests, the higher will be the motivation to resolve the conflict. Some textbooks and films in literature, science and social studies contain material that has the potential to be used in this manner. An important fact to keep in mind is that all of this reasoning is applied to some content area. Facts, principles and definitions still remain an essential part of the curriculum.

AN APPLICATION OF THE
EVALUATION OF MORAL EDUCATION

Just over two years ago, two Brookline, Massachusetts teachers, Margot Strom and Bill Parsons, received Title IV-C funds for a project entitled "Facing History and Ourselves:

Holocaust and Human Behavior." This curriculum unit is actually broader than a strictly moral education program. It includes involvement by art and music teachers and counselors. The European history it describes spans the first half of the twentieth century and almost none of it exists in the eighth grade social studies texts presently available.

The project fits naturally into a four unit sequence in the eighth grade social studies classes, which has as its theme Conflict and Resolution, with examples drawn from U.S. and World History. Both the Superintendent of Schools and the Director of Social Studies supported the unit enthusiastically. The principals of the schools where it was first introduced allowed many changes in established schedules to allow the art teacher and others to be present in the discusssions and expand the experience of the children into their own classes with lessons on propaganda posters, monuments, etc.

The unit begins with a forthright discussion of why students are being asked to study the Holocaust and why most teachers and textbooks avoid this painful subject. The students feel that this discussion is a powerful message of respect, that they are being admitted to the adult world and entrusted with its secrets. The classroom climate reinforces this equality between teacher and students and encourages them to express their opinions, knowing they will be heard respectfully. Students respond with increasing involvement and maturity.

Materials are designed for students entering the stage of early formal operations. They deal with real people and specific incidents. Students are asked to coordinate the different perspectives of victim, victimizer, leader, resistor, and bystander. In trying to make sense out of discrepant events, they debate interpretations and avoid overly simple explanations. The appreciation of multiple causality is an important goal of the unit. Eventually, students see their discussions focusing on issues or questions rather than facts.

A central issue is the question of individual responsibility in and for society. While this might be thought as too sophisticated for an eighth grade student, the issues are already in their minds. They see society as a large group and struggle daily with group issues, such as when to go along and when to resist, what they and their group believe in, when to betray their values for the group and vice versa, what risks they are willing to take.

Continual use of terms like society, individual, obedience, authority, responsibility and prejudice, whose meanings develop during the course, helps students to make connections between different parts of the unit and to relate it to events in their lives. History is presented as a tool for understanding human behavior, for discussions about Nazi tyranny are also about what happens in the school cafeteria. Students bring their own examples of peer group pressure to bear on stories about Germans who become Nazi soldiers.

The unit avoids traps involved in teaching such highly charged material by carefully preparing students to make sense out of readings or films that may be moving, frightening or shocking. They are given opportunities to share and build on each others' feelings, to talk about the issues and grapple with the questions.

While students at this point in development could easily identify with the aggressor and see the course as a way to manipulate power for self protection and enhancement, the focus on community and responsibility with an emphasis on first-person accounts presenting many perspectives make this likelihood minimal.

A variety of forms of documentation were gathered to show the presence of project, teacher, and student antecedents. These included letters and memos from administrators, records of workshops and conferences, and scores from reading tests administered the previous year.

Processes were recorded by the documentarian, especially with regard to dissemination, while logs kept by the teachers and data from classroom observation instruments showed that the desired processes such as student participation, a supportive atmosphere and an intellectually challenging discussion format were taking place.

Specific categories employed in observing videotapes of

classroom discussion included: establishing the classroom atmosphere; incorporating language skills; eliciting questions, past events, clarification, opinions and reasoning; encouraging perspective-taking; relating other experiences and lessons to this lesson; eliciting definitions or the use of abstract terms; generating conflict in discussion.

Frequency counts of behaviors or communications were combined with holistic judgments to determine the degree to which an appropriate discussion was actually taking place. It is this area where the line between transactions and outcomes becomes blurred, since many things said by some pupils or the teacher would constitute outcomes for them, but provide the means for other students to change their concept or reasoning of the issue at hand.

Outcomes of the project include the establishment of a resource center, a draft of the curriculum guide, slide presentations prepared by the art teacher, audio and video tapes of speakers and survivors, an established tie with the Armenian community (membership on the advisory council, books and films on the Armenian genocide) and the first steps in establishing a permanent Holocaust center.

Teachers expanded their techniques to include the developmental education methods of introducing cognitive conflict and resolution. Other eighth grade teachers expressed a willingness to teach the unit, and looked forward to working more closely with the extended staff in art, library and counseling. The extended staff gave workshops to their colleagues and contributed names of books, films, survivors, and scholars on the Holocaust for possible inclusion in the curriculum or the resource center.

During the first year of the project, the two authors taught the unit in their own schools. Since there was evidence from standardized test score data that there were ability (as measured in reading achievement) differences between the two schools, a control class from each was chosen in which another unit from the eighth grade curriculum was taught.

Both experimental and control classes were pre- and post-tested in four domains: knowledge and understanding of concepts and vocabulary; interpersonal awareness (Selman, 1974); moral reasoning (Kohlberg, 1969); and ego development (Loevinger, 1966).

A word about "history" as a threat to the internal validity of this evaluation design (Campbell and Stanley, 1963) is in order. The television series on the Holocaust was aired some weeks after the unit ended in the schools and after the post-tests were administered. In addition, record breaking snow-storms in January and February, 1978 in Boston caused sus-pension of classes for more than a week, but the effects were judged to be minimal.

The results of the social studies concepts, skills and vocab-ulary test showed the experimental group growing more in attaining these goals than the control group, especially in describing decisions made by individuals as members of a society. Large numbers of students in the unit classes were able to give adequate definitions or examples of vocabulary words, though there were some interesting confusions, such as Aryans and Armenians (terms probably never mentioned in the same class) and many students identified Nazis as sol-diers, rather than members of a political party.

Two of the developmental measures allowed both quanti-tative and qualitative analysis. Both interpersonal awareness and moral reasoning have continuous counterparts to their stage determination. In these scales, 100 corresponds to a pure Stage One response, 150 corresponds to a transitional state between Stages One and Two, etc.

Students in the program classes grew more on both mea-sures than did students in the control classes. An analysis of covariance with post-test score as the dependent variable and reading level and pre-test score as covariates was performed once the assumptions had been shown to hold for this data. The program group grew statistically significantly more in interpersonal awareness, mostly from Stage Two to a transi-tional state between Stage Two and Three, while the growth in moral reasoning over the control group could have been attributed to chance.

To respond to the concerns of developmental psychologists

that continuous measures and aggregate scores such as the mean offer little information that is useful to them, two qualitative analyses were performed which used proportions of subjects at each stage on both groups on both testings as the data. Then, by comparing cumulative distributions with the well known but seldom employed Kolmogorov-Smirnov non-parametric two sample test, the same hypotheses may be tested using procedures which maintain the integrity of the data. This analysis was performed on the global stage scores of each of the three developmental measures but only interpersonal awareness retained the significant difference favoring the program group.

Significant growth over that of the control group was evidenced on several issues within interpersonal awareness. Rule Orientation, Decision-Making/Organization, Leadership, Jealousy/Exclusion, Conflict Resolution, Termination and Global Score all showed more subjects in the experimental group reasoning at a more complex level, than in the control group.

A second analysis was performed to determine the proportion of subjects in both groups who showed a new stage of reasoning on the post-test not present in the pre-test. Here, too, there were several issues in interpersonal awareness where growth in the experimental groups exceeds the control group students.

Finally, an analysis of papers describing students' experiences in the unit, written after the unit ended, revealed much evidence of an understanding of more than one perspective on a dilemma, the ability to put oneself in another position, an ability to draw analogies in school life to the content in the unit, changes of attitudes toward minority groups, reduction of stereotyping, increased interest in personal history of parents and grandparents, awareness of cultural differences, and a willingness to express ideas in class without fear of ridicule. These themes were present in several students' papers and showed a sophistication not displayed in the other instruments.

As a result of workshops run by the two teacher-authors, sufficient interest has been generated in the district that in the summer following the initial year, all eighth grade social studies teachers, and the librarians, art teachers, etc., from each school participated in the project by including the unit in the social studies curriculum.

SUMMARY

The new directions referred to in the title of this paper are several; an incorporation of a sophisticated methodology of evaluation into work focusing on different dimensions than classical research activities; articulation of specific teacher and student behaviors that exemplify the practice of constructivist education; an increased clarity in the desired outcomes of moral education; the application of non-parametric statistics to maintain the integrity of data.

Many of the tools, knowledge and skills needed to proceed already exist, but probably not in any one of the growing numbers of people engaged in moral education. The success of this enterprise will be determined by the degree with which educators, psychologists and responsive statisticians can productively work together.

REFERENCES

Campbell, D. T., and Stanley, J. C. **Experimental and Quasi-Experimental Designs for Research**. Chicago: Rand and McNally, 1963.

Colby, A. "Values Clarification." *Harvard Educational Review*, 1975, 45, 134-143.

Cook, T. D., and Campbell, D. T. **Quasi Experimentation**. Chicago: Rand McNally, 1979.

Isaacs, N. **Children's Ways of Knowing**. New York: Teachers College Press, 1974.

Kohlberg, L. "Stage and Sequence: The Cognitive-Developmental Approach to Socialization." In D. A. Goslins (Ed.) **Handbook of Socialization Theory and Research**. Chicago: Rand McNally, 1969.

Kohlberg, L., and Mayer, R. "Development as the Aim of Education." *Harvard Educational Review*, 1972, 42, 449-496.

Kuhn, D. "The Application of Piaget's Theory of Cognitive Development to Education." *Harvard Educational Review*, 1979, 49, 340-360.

Loevinger, J. "The Meaning and Measurement of Ego Development." *American Psychologist*, 1966, 21, 195-206.

Mager, R. R. **Preparing Objectives for Programmed Instruction.** San Francisco: Fearson Press, 1962.

Marascuilo, L. A., and McSweeney, M. **Nonparametric and Distribution-Free Methods for the Social Sciences.** Monterey: Brooks/Cole, 1977.

Mayer, R. "Describing Children's Experiences in Theoretically Different Classrooms: An Observational Assessment of Four Early Education Curriculum Models." Unpublished doctoral thesis, Harvard University, 1973.

Popham, W. J. "Objectives and Instruction." In W. J. Popham, et al. (Eds.) **Instructional Objectives.** Chicago: Rand McNally, 1969.

Power. C., and Reimer, J. "Moral Atmosphere: An Educational Bridge Between Moral Judgment and Action." *New Directions in Child Development*, 1978, 2, 105-116.

Raths, L. E., Harmin, M., and Simon, S. B. **Values and Teaching.** Columbus: Merril Pub. Co., 1966.

Selman, R. "A Structural Analysis of Levels of Role-Taking in Middle Childhood." *Child Development*, 1974, 45, 803-807.

Siegel, S. **Nonparametric Statistics for the Behavioral Sciences.** New York: McGraw-Hill, 1956.

Simon, A. **Mirrors for Behavior.** Philadelphia: Research for Better Schools, 1970.

Chapter 3

CREATING A "MINDSET" FOR EVALUATING A LIBERAL ARTS CURRICULUM WHERE "VALUING" IS A MAJOR OUTCOME

Marcia Mentkowski

Recently, theorists and researchers who have contributed to our understanding of how moral reasoning develops in children and adults have begun to work together with practitioners. Several new directions emerge from this union. One is the challenge to embrace program evaluation as a necessary next step in the move from the abstract to integrating moral education goals in the total educational milieu. The purpose of this paper is to contribute to creating a "mindset" for evaluating moral education and programs with a values dimension.

When Lawrence Kohlberg initiated the Just Community approach to schooling, he made the leap from theory to practice. This step allowed a test of concepts emerging from his theory and research studies, and contributed to their credibility for the educational world. Some years after this leap to practice, Kohlberg confessed to the "psychologist's fallacy"[1] of assuming that stages of development could or should form the most important cornerstone of educational practice. This theorist's fallacy has its counterpart in the "researcher's fallacy," in which we are tempted to assume that the goals, methodology and instrumentation that are characteristic of research studies seeking theory development and demonstrating cause-effect relationships should form the cornerstone of an approach to the practice of evaluation.

While many program evaluation studies in current literature seem to depend almost entirely on the techniques of the researcher, evaluation has begun to emerge as a separate discipline. Other evaluators have evolved strategies that clearly recognize the differences between the purpose of research studies and those of evaluation,[2] and have created alternate approaches (Parlett & Hamilton, 1976). This development, together with the growing recognition that practitioners are equal partners in creating theory and practice in moral education (Mosher, 1977), sets the stage for avoiding the "researcher's fallacy."

A mindset for program evaluation thus begins with the awareness that evaluation goals and strategies are better selected and derived from the practitioner than from the theorist. The question is *not* "What is available that we can use to evaluate?" Rather,

"How might we best analyze the special characteristics of this specific moral or other developmental education curriculum so that our evaluation objectives match the nature of the specific program?"

"How can we best use the tools assessing cognitive structural development and other broad outcomes of a program, and instruments that assess the program's specific instructional objectives?"

"Will program evaluation instruments be used to credential or to diagnose student performance?"

Instruments which have been used for theory testing—even though they have demonstrated reliability and validity—need to be filtered first through the practitioner's goals, objectives, learning strategies and assessment processes. Once they emerge from this crucial dialectic, they may be effective program evaluation instruments as well.

One projected outcome of this move from theory-and-research to practice-and-evaluation is that we are encouraged to investigate questions suggested by practitioners in addition to those relating to moral reasoning and judgment. Elementary and secondary school educators, sensitive to the concerns of parents, school board members and community groups, are asking us as evaluators to attend to the relationship between moral judgment and moral behavior, and to examine program impacts on ethical systems which the child has been taught or which the adolescent has come to value.

A second direction enhanced by the move to practice involves our asking how moral development intervention strategies integrate with subject areas and contribute toward the development of other skills and abilities. Practitioners in higher education are developing curricula that are reviewed collaboratively by colleagues in a variety of disciplines. They emphasize not only growth in moral judgment about right and wrong, but also ask us to consider how values—the "nature of the good and the worthwhile"—are developed within their respective disciplines and demonstrated in pre-professional practice. Practitioners also urge us to investigate how analytical ability is enhanced, or how social interaction skills are developed, in discussions about moral issues.

A third direction arises in the practitioner's effort to intergrate moral development into the total learning milieu, mirrored in such labels as "civic education," "reasoning ability," "building community,"[3] and "the valuing process" (Earley, Mentkowski & Schafer, 1980). Whatever the term, the common understanding seems to be that moral development can be impacted by a created context which employs a variety of strategies to insure students' moral development, integrates this with other content areas and abilities, and impacts students' "patterns of action" (Power & Riemer, 1978). As evaluators, we face a considerable challenge in trying to weigh the effectiveness of such integrated environments and their several elements.

Still another important direction comes from institutions of higher education which make explicit the underlying objective of enhancing adult values and moral development. Liberal arts colleges are paralleling psychologists' efforts

(Gilligan & Murphy, 1979) to clarify the place and function of moral development across the life-span. Colleges of all types are responding to an influx of experienced, older adults who wish to achieve career change, upward mobility, or self-realization. Meanwhile, several professional schools and associations are re-emphasizing ethics and responsibility as a necessary corollary to professional expertise.

Finally, moral educators are beginning this emphasis on program evaluation at a time when all educators are holding themselves more accountable—to their own goals and standards, to students, and to other groups. Usually they expect to do so precisely through program evaluation. Couple this with an increased emphasis on standards rather than normative comparisons (e.g., competence-based education), and it is clear that we face an enormous complexity in evaluating moral education programs. How we approach this complexity as evaluators—our "mindset"—will impact our ability to respond to these questions effectively and to influence the future evolution of moral education in elementary, secondary, higher and professional education.

The plan of this chapter is to respond to this complexity by describing an approach to program evaluation at a liberal arts college where the development of valuing is an explicit outcome. The college is Alverno, a liberal arts institution for women, half of whose students are over traditional college age. Alverno embodies several of the new directions being taken by practitioners with a commitment to moral and values education, and has made it an explicit major goal of liberal education to produce graduates who are morally responsible.

The faculty has described value and moral development in terms of a process that includes moral *knowing, judging* and *acting*. They integrate development of this "valuing ability"[4] within the content of the traditional liberal arts disciplines. The valuing ability is also integrated with the development of these other explicitly defined outcomes:[5]

Effective communications ability

Analytical capability

Problem solving ability

Effective social interaction

Effectiveness in individual/environment relationships

Responsible involvement in the contemporary world

Aesthetic responsiveness

Valuing is thus integrated into the total learning milieu, and has been further identified as a critical ability in certain majors and professions, such as the development of professional and ethical responsibility in the nursing major (Alverno College Nursing Faculty, 1979).

The faculty came to consensus on the important outcomes of college in 1971. Since that time they have developed learning methods and assessments to teach toward and measure these abilities, with a heavy emphasis on creating opportunities for "experiential learning" (Doherty, Mentkowski & Conrad, 1978). In 1973, they implemented a "mastery-learning" or "outcome-centered" curriculum. Each of the eight outcomes is broken open into a learning sequence of six increasingly complex levels, each with multiple assessments. Students' demonstrations of these abilities—including valuing—are assessed repeatedly at each level according to criteria set by the faculty.

DERIVING EVALUATION PURPOSES
FROM CURRICULUM GOALS

An important step in evaluating "valuing" within such a curriculum is to clarify the purpose of program evaluation as a whole in relation to the broad goals of the curriculum, and to let the questions faculty asked in developing the curriculum be the source of the questions that guide evaluation. Letting curriculum values and goals guide those of evaluation sets the stage for avoiding the researcher's fallacy.

In creating their curriculum, Alverno faculty asked these questions:

What are the abilities each student must be able to demonstrate in order that we consider her liberally educated?

How can we develop these abilities in each student so that they become internalized, integrated and generalizable?

How will we know if each student has achieved these abilities according to our prescribed standards?

In establishing an Office of Evaluation, faculty asked these questions:

Is the learning process we use to develop abilities actually working the way we have designed it?

Are learning outcomes the result of instruction? Do they generalize across time and situations? Do outcomes reflect what we understand about students and their development and the nature of the abilities we are teaching toward?

How do the outcomes characteristic of our students compare with what is possible for them to achieve—both in regard to outcomes we credential and to the "intangible" outcomes of the college experience? Do abilities learned in college impact graduates' future performance?

The purposes of program evaluation, then, are threefold. First, evaluation of the learning process itself must *insure program quality*. In the same way that the assessment process diagnoses strengths and weaknesses of individual students, so the evaluation process must diagnose the program's strengths and weaknesses.

A second purpose of evaluation is to *insure program effectiveness* by demonstrating the extent to which learning outcomes are the result of the learning process, i.e., of instruction. Evaluating students' abilities across time and situations examines transfer and generalizability and contributes to the construct validity of the abilities, as well as to faculty's understanding of how the abilities develop in students. These two program evaluation purposes—evaluating the learning process to achieve quality assurance and evaluating the effect of instruction on learning outcomes—insure the internal validity of the curriculum.

Establishing internal validity sets the stage for the third purpose of evaluation: to *insure program validity*. Historically, this has usually meant comparing students against instruments that provide normative comparisons for certain curriculum outcomes, like the well-known College Board battery. For Alverno, establishing external validity means that faculty hold themselves accountable not only to standards they have set but also to those implied in their students' and society's expectations—as well as to standards set by more general visions of human potential.

Alverno faculty recognize that in some ways, of course, they cannot credential development. They will not withhold a student's graduation because she has achieved less than either her own or their vision of what is possible in personal maturity or developmental "stage." Faculty do credential certain measurable aspects of the abilities included in these "intangible" outcomes, and they only credential what they have seen the student demonstrate in the "created context" of the undergraduate experience.

Yet faculty help to establish the validity of their curriculum when they hold it to the more "intangible" or external standards. "To what extent," faculty have asked us to investigate, "do we contribute to the developmental gains of each student in ego, moral, and intellectual development? To what extent do we meet her expectations for her own growth and development? To what extent does the curriculum impact her future performance as a person and a professional?"

Evaluating the Valuing Ability

Within our total evaluation of the Alverno curriculum, we look at each of the abilities identified by the faculty as outcomes. Since valuing is one of these eight abilities, the overall curriculum goals and general evaluation purposes hold for it as well as for the others. The specific goals and methods relevant to the "valuing education" dimension of Alverno's curriculum provide a case study in the "mindset" and methods needed to evaluate moral education.

Insuring Program Quality

Program evaluation methods for insuring the quality of learning strategies and assessment techniques can be best understood by briefly reviewing the curriculum structures for teaching and assessing the valuing ability.

In the early seventies, when the faculty synthesized goals from each academic discipline into the broad outcomes or competence areas of liberal education, they charged an Academic Task Force with elaborating each competence into more teachable detail.[6] Thus, the valuing ability is set forth in a "learning sequence" of six pedagogical levels, in which the student moves from relatively simple to more complex demonstrations of the valuing ability:[7]

Identifying own values

Inferring and analyzing values in artistic and humanistic works

Relating values to scientific and technological developments

Engaging in valuing in decision-making in multiple contexts

Analyzing and formulating the value foundation of a specific area of knowledge, in its theory and practice.

Applying own theory of value and the value foundation of an area of knowledge in a professional context

Each student must demonstrate the first four basic levels of the ability, and then may or may not work at the fifth or sixth levels of the sequence depending on the demands of her major. Mastery of one level must be credentialed before she can proceed to the next.

Given a description of the pedagogical levels and the general performance criteria by which a student will be assessed and credentialed at each level, each faculty member analyzes his/her course and decides where and in what ways the course contributes most naturally to the development of the valuing ability, and how student achievement of the competence can best be demonstrated and assessed. In this semester's course offerings (Fall, 1979), forty-five instructors are teaching toward the valuing ability in fifty-two courses, in each of Alverno's fourteen academic and professional departments. This means that in a given semester, about half the faculty invite students to contract to develop valuing as an explicit course outcome. Other faculty teach valuing as well, even though it may not be an explicit course outcome, and all instructors participate in faculty development workshops on valuing.

A first step in insuring the quality of teaching and assessing for the valuing ability is to create certain review procedures. Several procedures had already been established by the faculty as ways to formalize their inquiry into this new area of educational practice to which they had committed themselves. Rather than establish competing or redundant procedures, the Office of Evaluation incorporated these where possible into the overall process of program evaluation.

The syllabus review process is a case in point. The **Faculty Handbook on Learning and Assessment** (1977) describes the meaning of "valuing" at each level and the relationship to other levels, the general criteria for student achievement at each level, the assessment process, sample learning experiences, and the significant relationship of valuing to other competences. Developing a course syllabus in which a student contracts for one or more levels of valuing means integrating these broad outcomes and criteria within the content of a particular course structure. Syllabi are reviewed by a faculty committee against established criteria for clarity and effectiveness, and by departments. Assessment instruments must likewise meet criteria established by the faculty. A special review committee—consisting of a representative group of faculty and staff who have developed expertise in assessment design, administration and validation—gives feedback to departments on their instruments and conducts workshops for faculty on improving instruments.

These processes help us to evaluate the extent to which teaching and assessment meet standards set by faculty based on years of expertise in teaching and assessing. The faculty have also created another structure for insuring the quality of the learning process. For each of the eight major learning outcomes, a "Competence Division" has been created to function much like the traditional discipline departments. The Valuing Competence Division,[8] made up of faculty volunteers from various disciplines, takes primary responsibility for the continual refinement and reconceptualization of the valuing process and of how it is taught and assessed. They monitor the literature and ongoing programs nationwide. They meet regularly to refine the specifications for each level, and division members participate in interdisciplinary reviews of course designs, teaching/learning strategies and assessment methods. It is their responsibility to constantly monitor teaching and assessing of valuing throughout the college. This group of "experts on valuing" provides a source for insuring the quality of teaching and assessment. It functions diagnostically, holding faculty to the continuously evolving standards created by their developing expertise.

Examples from the work of the Valuing Division illustrate evaluation strategies for insuring quality of teaching and assessing. For instance, Division members co-assess some levels of valuing, especially at the higher levels, by participating in the actual assessment process. They are present during the assessment, observe how the assessment is carried out, and actually co-assess—that is, review student performance against the established criteria. Along with other assessors, they can directly observe the administration of the instrument and the range of students' responses. Division members may also collect samples of student performance from several disciplines at a particular level and review them against the criteria for that level. This lets them check on the extent to which student performance is actually meeting college-wide criteria, and serves as a source of information for evaluating and revising a particular instrument.

A second example occurs as the Division creates tools to' evaluate the quality of teaching methods and instructor behavior. Criteria have been developed, for instance, to judge the extent to which a proposed "moral dilemma" yields the necessary ingredients for an effective discussion. Division members have also created criteria for evaluating a facilitator's effectiveness in a moral dilemma discussion.[9] Moral discussions are videotaped and Division members, together with the instructor conducting the discussion, rate the extent to which the facilitator "stretches student thinking, creates conflict, varies the dilemma circumstances, promotes analysis of student reasoning," etc. Meeting these criteria is critical when moral discussions are part of student assessment. The instrument will not be effective if the "stimulus"—the moral discussion—is not effective or reliable. Indeed, faculty have disregarded data from some assessments when the discussion did not create an adequate opportunity for students to demonstrate the several skills involved.

In the work of the Valuing Competence Division outlined above, expert judgment functions as an important program evaluation technique. Faculty members judge teaching methods and assessment tools against criteria that have been set by consensus and have been explicitly detailed. These criteria come from a variety of sources, but most have been generated from years of experience teaching and assessing students. Such program evaluation, whether carried out formally against explicit criteria or more informally against more intuitive criteria, is diagnostic and illuminative.[10] It involves the total faculty through built-in faculty groups and functions which allow instructors the constant opportunity to stand back from a particular curriculum component— syllabus, assessment tool, teaching method—and judge its quality. The same faculty expertise that assesses student performance thus consistently evaluates all aspects of the curriculum. This diagnostic, experience-based function creates a changing, dynamic curriculum. It is the base on which the credibility of the practitioner rests. Formalized and systematic opportunities for program evaluation carried out by the Office of Evaluation with explicit, public criteria enhance this process.

Insuring Program Effectiveness

The educator asks of a curriculum, a learning strategy, or even a diagnostic assessment tool: "Is the 'Intervention' working? Are students able to do what they could not do before the intervention?" For a performance-based, outcome-centered curriculum, this question is critical.

Alverno has approached the complexity of this challenge by creating a college-wide "assessment process"[11] that uses numerous multi-dimensional methods of observing and recording a student's abilities in action. (Throughout this paper, the terms "assessment" and "assess" are reserved to refer to this part of the curriculum while "evaluation" and "evaluate" refer to program evaluation under the auspices of the Office of Evaluation.) Assessment criteria and techniques are public and explicit. About seventy-five percent of a student's assessments occur in her courses. They often include traditional measures of course outcomes, but instructors integrate these with criteria specific to the competences being demonstrated and also employ multi-method, innovative and eclectic tools. In addition, the Assessment Center (equipped with a TV studio, two-way mirrors and other facilities) allows measurement of student progress at each curriculum level across time, external to instruction. The assessment process thus allows each student's developing abilities to be assessed by a variety of persons, in multiple contexts, across a number of instances, in the settings where they have been learned and in new situations, across content areas, with and without a specific stimulus, and "on the spot" in field experiences.

While the major purpose of the assessment process is to credential the individual student's progress at each curriculum level, it is also designed to diagnose strengths and weaknesses and to provide her with structured feedback, an opportunity for self-evaluation, and further learning prescriptions. Because the curriculum is structured as a series of sequential pedagogical levels, demanding mastery of one level before proceeding to the next, the assessment process provides built-in checkpoints of the student's progress, continuously yielding data to faculty on the extent to which each student is meeting curriculum objectives. Approximately 90 instruments are currently in use to assess student progress in the valuing ability.[12]

Thus the assessment process, with its built-in structures for insuring reliability and validity, provides a data base for evaluating the effects of instruction on student performance. Then, as the Valuing Division reviews assessment techniques or analyzes cross-disciplinary samples of student performance at a particular level, they raise questions about the validity of both the assessment techniques and the construct of "the valuing ability." Division members have asked:

"How best can we use group data from student performance on our instruments to test our assumptions about the complex nature of the valuing ability?"

"How can we be sure that each aspect of the competence is measured in all its complexity?"

"How can we be sure that aspects common to valuing across disciplines are measured in each discipline?"

"How best do we assess the extent to which our learning sequence in valuing is indeed sequential in complexity?"

"Do we actually ask students to demonstrate more sophisticated aspects of valuing—or does it just look more complex at the upper levels because of integration with more complex content?"

"How can we improve our understanding of how the valuing ability develops in students?"

"How is valuing different from or similar to problem solving? to social interaction? to analysis? or other outcomes we have identified?"

Our work in evaluating the effects of instruction is considerably enhanced both by the assessment process built into the Alverno curriculum, and by the Valuing Division's ongoing critique of the assessment process as it is used to credential student development in valuing. The assessment process itself gives us a rich and detailed data base on student performance at all levels and in all settings throughout the college. The Valuing Division's questions provide focus for our own inquiry as evaluators into the effectiveness not only of instruction but also of assessment—the college-wide process and its specific tools.

CREATING A GENERIC EVALUATION INSTRUMENT
WITH ASSESSMENT INSTRUMENT CHARACTERISTICS

Our "mindset" for program evaluation insists that evaluation purposes be derived from curriculum goals. Similarly, our evaluation instruments must reflect the general characteristics of the faculty's techniques for assessing student performance if we are to accurately critique instructional effectiveness. We must resist the temptation to import a ready-made instrument currently available to assess moral judgment or values and simply adopt it as an evaluation tool.

An evaluation instrument, like an assessment instrument, must have the following characteristics:

> The stimulus must be valid in that it measures the learning objectives for each level of valuing.

> It must elicit the full nature of the valuing ability—knowing, judging and acting—a holistic process.

> It must allow an opportunity to integrate content at an appropriate level of sophistication.

> It must allow measurement of the integration of valuing with other relevant abilities such as analysis and comminications.

> It should be designed as a *production* task rather than a *recognition* task.

Its mode must be similar to the ability as usually expressed, rather than an artificial mode (such as ranking statements).

It will most likely be subjectively scored, by more than one assessor, against objective criteria.

It should be administered externally to the learning situation—preferably in the Assessment Center.

It should be diagnostic, since the student has come to expect structured feedback as an instrinsic part of every experience in which the college asks her to demonstrate her abilities.

It should provide evidence for credentialing the student's performance.

By measuring the valuing ability, it is particularly important to distinguish between evidence used for diagnostic purposes and that used to credential. Evaluation instruments should provide the kind of evidence of the valuing ability that the faculty is willing to credential, in order to corroborate or challenge student performance already credentialed. Although faculty will credential the extent to which a student provides analytically-based reasons for her judgments, they will not credential a student's stage of moral reasoning. Faculty will not credential her values, but will credential her ability to state them or compare and contrast them with other value systems. At the same time, program evaluation instruments should and do provide evidence of development beyond what can be credentialed. We as evaluators are interested in monitoring a student's reasoning ability, or the relationship of her judgments to her behavior, even though these may not always be amenable to credentialing. Faculty, too, are always interested in diagnosing more aspects of the student's development—in the valuing process as in any other area—than they can credential.

On the other hand, evaluation does impose some unique demands. For example, although the nature of the ability being assessed lends itself to qualitative judgment, an evaluation instrument should provide numerical scores so that it can be more readily validated or used for cross-college comparisons. It must also measure all levels aready credentialed.

Two years ago, the Valuing Division joined with the Assessment Committee (charged with the college-wide evaluation, revision, and validation of assessment instruments) to develop a "generic" instrument that would examine student performance across curriculum levels of valuing. The result was an additional instrument—a "generic criterion measure"—to assess levels 1 through 4, which all students would demonstrate at the end of their general education sequence. Because its content and setting were external to any of the student's course experiences, this instrument was expected to provide a summative assessment of her development in valuing to this point.

The instrument's externality also gave it potential usefulness as a program evaluation tool. It is an unusual kind of external criterion measure in that it reiterates every one of the criteria by which the student's several instructors have assessed her developing ability. Yet it applies them as part of a tool which is in no way dependent upon the specific assessments or courses she has taken.

Space does not permit more than a brief description of this generic evaluation instrument.[13] It consists of four parts that ask the student 1) to infer values from a literary work; 2) to analyze the relationship of values to scientific and technological developments; 3) to participate in a moral dilemma group discussion; and 4) to analyze her own decision-making process. Various sets of stimuli can be developed for the instrument, reflecting a range of issues. One such set involves students in the issue of genetic engineering—using a short story, a newspaper article and an article from a scientific journal, a moral dilemma, and directions for her response to each. She is first asked to compare the values she infers from the short story to her own value system, and then to that of American society. She then writes an editorial for either the local newspaper or a scientific journal on "How our decisions regarding scientific developments influence our value systems, cause value conflict, and raise questions regarding the relationship between private decision-making and public policy." She next participates in a facilitator-led small group discussion of a moral dilemma, and then analyzes her own decision-making process throughout the experience and writes a letter to a congressman on genetic screening "stating her case, describing her action plan and relating how her own values motivated her decision."

The student's performance is measured according to 67 criteria in all:

> 29 of these repeat the faculty's criteria from levels 1 through 4 on which she has already been wholly or partly credentialed;

> 21 were developed by the Valuing Division for the student's self-assessment on the moral discussion; and

> 17 were developed by the Division for instructor assessment of the student's participation in the moral discussion and for tallying the occurrence of her use of the various modes of judgment, her identifying of moral issues and moral orientations categorized in Kohlberg et al., **Standard Form Scoring Manual (1978)**.

The student is credentialed on the 29 "level" criteria. The 17 criteria for judging her performance in the discussion also help form a basis for credentialing judgments on some of those 29 criteria, such as "Recognizes necessity for and utilizes information and knowledge in moral reasoning, judging and deciding" or "Articulates the point of view of another person or position with empathy and reason." The Kohlberg modes, issues and orientations used in this generic instrument are most useful *not* for "staging" or credentialing the student, but for helping to identify the issues she uses in the discussion and her orientation toward them, as well as the extent to which she employs predominant judgment modes.

The 21 criteria by which the student assesses herself are one source of diagnostic feedback for the student. Instructors provide structured feedback on the 29 level criteria in conjunction with a joint review of her self-assessment. We are also beginning to use the 17 criteria effectively in this manner, as a way to give diagnostic feedback on student participation in the discussion and to assist her in identifying which mode of judgment or dominant orientation she is likely to use in resolving moral dilemmas.

What has been created in this "generic" instrument is an opportunity to elicit and examine the moral reasoning of college students in several situations, to view and analyze their participation in a moral dilemma discussion and to judge the discussion's effectiveness. It allows us as evaluators to measure the outcome of two years of college instruction aimed at developing the valuing ability, for all areas of the curriculum as well as for the program as a whole.

Validating the Generic Evaluation Instrument

The Office of Evaluation conducted a pre-instruction/post-instruction comparison study. We administered the generic criterion instrument to a pre-instruction group of students just entering college (who were about 10 years older on the average than the post-instruction group, to control for the effects of life experience), and to a post-instruction group credentialed at level 4 after two years in college. Results indicated that the post-instruction group performed significantly better as measured by the 29 "level" criteria from the generic instrument than the pre-instruction group. Each of the criteria was compared to identify those that discriminated the pre- and post-instruction groups. Correlational analyses were used to investigate the extent to which the 4 levels are actually sequential. Results indicated different patterns of response between the pre- and post-instruction groups, in that the instructed group demonstrated clusters of relationships among scores on the criteria and the pre-instruction group appeared to perform in a randomly scattered manner, indicating effectiveness of instruction (Friedman & Mentkowski, 1980).

Several of the results provide information for further revision of the instrument. The Valuing Division is currently extending the use of the instrument in the college, and has some plans to institute it college-wide through the Assessment Center. Analysis of the data gave us further insights into the nature of the ability and students' performance at Level 4. While the instrument is available to persons outside the college for the asking, we would *not* encourage other colleges to *adopt* this instrument. It has been developed to assess learning objectives particular to this curriculum. Further, since the instrument will be continually revised as we understand more about valuing, we can never claim it to be totally validated. Rather, the Office of Evaluation will work closely with the Division to identify questions for further analysis.

Insuring Program Validity

The evaluation methods described that insure the quality and effectiveness of the curriculum were primarily designed to be diagnostic and illuminative. In most cases, faculty establish the *internal validity* of the program by evaluating both the learning process and outcomes against standards developed in various Discipline and Competence Divisions and from observation and analysis of student performance on assessments.

Ultimately, however, faculty turn their attention to questioning the program's *external validity*. Here again, the goals of the curriculum influence how validity is demonstrated. At Alverno, the focus is on student development. In an outcome-centered curriculum, a student is assessed against standards, rather than against other students' normative performance (criterion vs. norm referenced). Consequently, faculty first ask of the evaluator:

> "How do the outcomes characteristic of our students
> compare with their potential—with what is possible
> for them to achieve?"

Faculty apply this question to the abilities they credential and to the "intangible" outcomes of the college experience promised to graduates by most liberal arts colleges (e.g. continued life-span development, transition to "life after college," self-directed and integrated personal functioning and life-long learning).

The contributions of theorist and researcher can have a major impact on how this first question challenging the program's external validity is investigated. One contribution from developmental psychologists is the description of broad developmental domains that can be measured, such as Kohlberg (1976), moral development; Loevinger (1970), ego development; Piaget (1972), cognitive development; and Perry (1968), intellectual and ethical development. These theorists provide us with a partial picture of students' potential for growth—and some of the criteria against which faculty can validate the non-credentialed outcomes of the curriculum. The cognitive-developmental instruments measuring these domains yield developmental norms that describe potential and, when used as external criterion measures, reflect on a program's adequacy (in contrast to comparisons with norms derived from averaging or percentile rank).

A second evaluation objective stems from the student-centered nature of the curriculum, as faculty ask:

> "Are outcomes we assess diagnostically and credential mirrored in students' perceptions of their developing abilities?"

A primary assumption is that integration, internalization and transfer of student abilities can be validated to some degree by tapping students' perceptions of their own growth and development. If students are aware of their abilities and have internalized them, they will refer to them spontaneously and use them to organize their experiences.

The developmental theorists contribute to investigating the second objective by showing us how to elicit and analyze cognitive processes as they occur—to assess the thinker in action. Piaget's, Kohlberg's and Perry's basic measurement strategy has been the interview (Loevinger's measure is a production task of completing sentences).

A third objective for establishing program validity comes from the faculty's view of college as a catalyst for life-long development:

"Are abilities learned in college related to the future personal and professional performance of graduates?"

Here, too, a developmental framework cautions us that abilities learned in college may not be visible in the same form in later years. The predictive validity of valuing may be difficult to establish if we simply look for "more of the same" in a follow-up study of graduates.

Deriving Evaluation Designs from Curriculum Structure

Given these objectives and a developmental "mindset," we select evaluation designs from curriculum structures. Rather than equate program success with average gains, faculty are interested in the extent to which the program is effective with each student. The valuing curriculum may facilitate growth only for students who are verbally skilled. Or students who enter college with already sophisticated abilities may coast through a curriculum and make few if any gains. With the focus on describing individual patterns of change and growth, faculty designed the curriculum to allow consecutive assessments throughout a student's college career. Consequently, in investigating the first objective ("How do outcomes compare with potential?") we are likely to select similar longitudinal designs. While longitudinal studies using external criterion measures are time-consuming and costly, they yield individual growth patterns. We have found it important not to rely too heavily on cross-sectional studies comparing entering students with graduates. On some measures, consecutive entering classes have performed in significantly different patterns.

For now, we have abandoned experimental designs for establishing both program effectiveness and validity. First, since all students complete at least four levels of the learning sequence, there are no control groups. In addition, faculty who may not explicitly invite students to contract for a particular ability are aware of it and may still teach it implicitly. We have begun to compare students who complete four levels in valuing with those who go on to Levels 5 and 6 because of their major field, but the currently available external criterion measures, for the most part, measure only one part of the complexity of the valuing process to be demonstrated at Level 6. Finally, selecting a control college is impractical. We cannot really "prove" a constantly changing and evolving curriculum by using the experimental model.

We do, however, have an opportunity to control for the effects of life experience on student outcomes and so can directly measure the effects of college on student performance. When the outcomes we study are developmental, we must control for development that occurs whether or not a person is enrolled in college. Fortunately, we have a large adult population, most of whom attend college full-time (achieving the same degree in four years) during a special schedule on weekends. Students enter Weekend College at a median age of 33 years in comparison to 22 years in the Weekday College. Consequently, we are able to compare gains in students' development in college against the effects of approximately 10 years of life experience. Longitudinal studies of women in the Weekend College also provide us with an opportunity to measure developmental gains well into adulthood.

One advantage of using criterion measures that have achieved some reputation (see next section) is that other colleges are also participating to some extent in collecting data on students. We are members of a consortium of colleges and cooperate with McBer and Company of Boston (headed by David McClelland), who have administered many of the instruments we use as external criterion measures to students at a range of colleges and universities with both highly selective and more open admission practices. James Rest (1979) has maintained a clearing-house on Defining Issues Test data which we find useful in comparing gains of Alverno students with those at other colleges. How Alverno students as a group compare normatively to students at other colleges receives less emphasis than how our students' individual gains over four years compare against (1) cognitive-developmental norms, and other standards derived from the faculty's understanding of the abilities they teach toward, and (2) students' perceptions of their own growth. Given these designs, we have selected external criterion instruments that most nearly approximate the measurement of the eight abilities that we teach toward, including valuing.

Choosing Instruments for Establishing Program Validity

Traditional measures of college outcomes have come under fire as measuring knowledge without performance, and as unrelated to future performance after college (McClelland, 1973). In fact, we have not been able to identify any one external criterion measure that provides a perfect match to any of the abilities we are validating. Given our criteria for instrument characteristics, particularly our insistence that they should be production tasks in order to measure the learner in action, few measures meet either the demands for the holistic nature of the ability or the mode of measurement. Consequently, we have selected instruments that assess broad outcomes of the curriculum. We have found that internal validation is best carried out with specific instrumentation, and external validation with measures of broad outcomes which also allow evaluation of one ability in relation to others. The cognitive-developmental measures, and recently developed measures of the expected outcomes of college (selected or developed by McBer and Company), have more nearly met our criteria for instruments, and allow us to "talk to" researchers and theorists outside the college through the common language of test scores and quantitative results.

In response to the question "How do the outcomes characteristic of our students compare with their potential?" we have identified the following objectives:[14]

(A) Assess students on *cognitive-developmental external criterion measures* identified as descriptive of individuals who have reached various levels of potential in ego, moral and intellectual development.[15]

  Test of Cognitive Development (after Piaget)

  Loevinger's Sentence Completion Test, a measure of ego development

  Kohlberg's Moral Judgment Instrument (written mode)

  Rest's Defining Issues Test

  Knefelkamp and Widick's Measure of Vocational, Educational and Personal Issues (after Perry)

(B) Assess students on *generic competence external criterion measures* that assess a variety of analytic and interpersonal abilities.[16]

  Kolb's Learning Style Inventory

  The Picture Story Exercise, scored for Stewart's Measures of Self-Definition and Stages of Adaptation

  Stewart and Winter's Analysis of Argument

  Winter's Test of Thematic Analysis

  Klemp and Connelly's Life History Exercise

  Kolb's Adaptive Style Inventory

  Watson-Glaser Test of Critical Thinking

The research design calls for a cross-sectional comparison of graduating seniors with entering freshmen on this battery of instruments, as well as a longitudinal study of two consecutive classes assessed when they enter, at midpoint, and when they graduate. While data collection is still in progress, the first longitudinal group will be complete in spring, 1980, with three consecutive measures per student on each instrument.

We have conducted total sampling of the two entering classes and one graduating class to reduce the impact of attrition on the longitudinal studies. For the purposes of this chapter, I will comment only on the cognitive-developmental instruments. Clearly, the instruments listed under the first objective more nearly relate to evaluation of the valuing ability, especially Kohlberg's Moral Judgment Instrument and Rest's Defining Issues Test.

Scoring this large number of production instruments is beyond the evaluation facilities of a liberal arts college. Our validation work is supported by a three-year grant from the National Institute of Education. Scoring is handled in three ways: training our own scoring teams (Loevinger's Sentence Completion Test and the Measure of Vocational, Educational and Personal Issues), using computer scoring (Defining Issues Test), and collaborating with consultants (Center for Moral Education at Harvard for the Kohlberg Moral Judgment Instrument). The advantages of production-type tasks are somewhat offset by the amount of scoring time, learning to score, and the consequent costs. Because we have a somewhat similar measure in the Defining Issues Test, we are administering the Moral Judgment Instrument to a sample of the students rather than the total group to cut costs. Scoring the Measure of Vocational, Educational and Personal Issues has entailed development work on the scoring system with materials and assistance from Lee Knefelkamp; scorers of the Sentence Completion Test have attended two scoring workshops conducted by Loevinger.

We worry about the effects of consecutive testing using the same instruments, although the cognitive-developmental instruments seem somewhat impervious to "faking" (Rest, 1976). But these production-task instruments have one clear advantage: they can be rescored in the future, an important characteristic for longitudinal studies where a more sophisticated understanding of the ability can be used to make better sense of data collected earlier (Colby, 1978).

While our data are still being collected and analyzed, we have some preliminary indications that when our traditional-aged students enter Weekday College, they are at Loevinger's Stage 3/4, Kohlberg's Stage 3 and Perry's Position 2/3. On Rest's recognition task, the Defining Issues Test (DIT), entering weekday students show significantly lower scores than do older students entering the Weekend College—but the latter group show significantly lower scores than graduating weekday seniors, who are much younger. For the production tasks measuring the Kohlberg, Loevinger and Perry stages, entering students in the Weekday College are significantly lower in stage than graduating seniors, who do not significantly differ from older Weekend College entering students.

While it would be premature to report statistics or other quantitative results, one hypothesis is that student's developmental gains show first on recognition tasks, and later on production tasks where the student must generate a response rather than recognize it. This is supported by our longitudinal results. After two years in both the Weekday and Weekend College, students show significant gains on the DIT, but not on the Moral Judgment Instrument.

In sum, though the instruments are time-consuming to score, necessitating long training, consensus scoring and a continuous struggle to maintain scorer reliability, we are creating a data bank that we believe will provide us with base-line developmental norms for use at Alverno and other colleges to establish program validity and to stimulate program development. We also look forward to opportunities to compare student performance on our own measures in valuing (particularly our generic instrument) with performance on the developmental measures. We do keep in mind, however, that these measures of moral judgment are but one aspect of how we have defined the valuing ability.

The Student Profile Study

The second external validity evaluation objective is to weigh the extent to which student outcomes of the college experience, including valuing, are shared perceptions of the students themselves. In response to the question "Are outcomes we assess diagnostically and credential mirrored in students' perceptions of their developing abilities?" a semi-structured interview is conducted with a sample of students from each class who complete the instruments just mentioned. This interview (Mentkowski & Much, 1980) is administered each spring as students move through college. The interviewer asks students to reflect on the past year by commenting on their learning experiences and their own development, to give students an opportunity to "speak for themselves" about their college experiences. We are particularly interested in how these perspectives change over four years in college and on into their professional lives. (The interview will form the basis for the follow-up interview of graduates in spring 1980, in response to the third evaluation objective, "Are abilities learned in college related to the future personal and professional performance of graduates?")

These interviews are incredibly rich in data and meaning, and provide a spontaneous measure of outcomes of the college experience. We developed the interview primarily because we knew we could not (nor did we want to) reduce what we might learn about students to test scores or even stages of development. We are most interested in assessing change and transition, and are challenged to describe the dialectical learning process that takes place as the student moves through college and interacts with the total learning milieu. While cognitive-developmental test scores may describe what she can do when she enters, at midpoint and when she leaves, we must also ask "How does it happen?"

Analysis of the interviews begins with identifying a general outcome for measurement, such as "student expectations and satisfactions," "perceptions of learning," "conflict and its resolution," or "the valuing ability." First, the investigator extracts all the relevant data from the transcribed interviews, and then does an "ethnographic" (Geertz, 1973) or interpretive analysis aimed at qualitative explication of the students' understandings of their learning experiences. At some point, we may attempt an explanation of these student experiences in terms of cognitive-developmental theory. For the moment, however, we are interested in a theory-independent description of *what there is* in the way of patterns to be explained.

Currently, we are working on a description of "the valuing ability" as found in the interview material. We are interested in what meaning the valuing ability has for the student. Does she speak of it as part of her approach to situations at school or in her personal life? When she refers to "using valuing," what kinds of examples does she give? While our ethnographic analysis is in progress, examples from the interviews illustrate the kind of data that emerges. The following statements should not be interpreted as either generally descriptive or common, but they begin to give some idea of the richness of the interview material.

First, there are many examples of increasing awareness of "the valuing ability," and a more in-depth awareness and self-conscious creation of "my own philosophy." Students seem to show increased objectivity and an enhanced ability to analyze, describe and critique their own and other ethical systems—including Alverno's. Additional outcomes such as transfer across settings and integration with other abilities seem to emerge as they describe their continual enacting of their values and judgments. They comment often on their growing ability to effect value and moral choices in professional situations. Through careful analysis of these interviews we hope to infer some of the "causes" of this increased growth students perceive.

These interviews, and the information from the battery of developmental instruments, provide us with an opportunity to develop case studies which will provide a context for the numbers.[17] One case study developed as a test provided information on the particular conflicts experienced by a student over a three year period. Her interviews provided a rich tapestry of explanation for major shifts in development reflected on the Defining Issues Test, the Loevinger Sentence Completion Test, the Kohlberg Moral Judgment Instrument, and the Perry measure. Listening to the student's own reflections about "How I changed and why" gave us a feel for the transitions she experienced from her point of view. We see this as an opportunity to understand other aspects of her development, and to identify clues from the learning milieu that may have been causal variables.

Jennifer speaks at the end of her freshman year:

"In my psychology course I just recently did valuing. I think that was very influential. Like for my valuing concept I took a comparison of how the values in the 1700's have influenced the concepts of adolescence from then to the present and I showed how values differ. Many people could go through a psychology course and unless they realize that values really play an important role in this changing concept, they could have missed that whole business going on there."

Jennifer in the spring of her sophomore year:

"I had this experience with _____, it was something that I cannot comprehend or understand. And when I faced this, I was totally forced to reevaluate everything inside of me and all my morals and all my values and every way I thought. I sat and listened to other people, and that too totally forced me to reevaluate myself. As I interacted with other people to figure out where I stood, I heard myself talking about it and that made me reprocess it and think my ideas over again until finally I was able to face that situation again and say, 'This is my position, this is where I stand'."

Jennifer after her junior year:

"I've done a lot (of valuing) in relation to nursing: working with suicidal people this year, counseling runaway teenagers that have been abused. In my past I guess I was guarded—this year I have been involved with it—I have grown so much. All of them were new experiences. I had to look at my values and say, 'Is this the way I believe?' or 'How do I believe?' or 'What is my philosophy here?' I guess you have to deal with conflict; when I am reevaluating my values there is always some kind of conflict and I have to go one way or another."

Interviews allow a broader sampling of a student's experience to emerge. As an evaluation resource, they can not be underestimated. Despite the cost and time of data collection and analysis, they provide us with the only index that can be used in all three evaluation functions: insuring program quality, evaluating the effects of the curriculum on students, and validating the curriculum. Further, they provide us with a method for recognizing the importance of the student's perspectives through other means than our attitude surveys and student course evaluations. The method also gives the student an opportunity for active collaboration in the research, and so protects her self-esteem.

JUSTICE IN EVALUATION

As developmental psychologist turned evaluator, it soon became apparent to me that "justice in evaluation" (House, 1976) meant insuring the self-esteem of the participants, recognizing the rights of the students and faculty involved in the evaluation, and providing feedback and benefits to both groups. Student participants expect to benefit from participating in the evaluation process and are regularly updated on the outcomes of the studies via "feedback" letters. Their self-esteem is critical, and I have met with student participants regularly to answer questions and provide a rationale for the instruments they complete. The rights of faculty to involvement in evaluation are recognized by their having equal opportunity with the evaluator to generate questions and interpret the data with full recognition that there are still other "ways of knowing" than those included in a systematic program evaluation. The information generated from formal evaluation and research studies is never "the whole truth" or "all that could be said," and faculty play a crucial role in determining the extent to which results have any meaning for the practice we try to improve. "Justice in evaluation" not only means recognizing the conflicting claims of various persons involved in the evaluation, it creates a much different atmosphere and tone for evaluation than that of research as

I have known it in my 15 years of involvement in more traditional sites and roles (Mentkowski, 1977).

This discussion of our approaches to evaluating valuing in a total curriculum to establish program quality, effectiveness and validity illustrates the tentativeness of our forays into evaluation, and the caution with which we approach establishing program validity. We employ multiple tools, aggregate research methods and "triangulation" with frequent cross-checking to see if results from one source are confirmed in another (Scriven, 1976). Our experiences have confirmed our view of evaluation as "process." While we hold little hope for "final" results, we have great expectations for contributing to ongoing program development and to the faculty's collective sense of "Who is the student?" and "How can we best facilitate her development?"

REFERENCE NOTES

1. Refer to Kohlberg's comments in the foreword to the following book: Hersh, R., Paolitto, D., & Reimer, J. **Promoting Moral Growth from Piaget to Kohlberg.** New York: Longman, 1979.

2. Refer to two recent volumes: Glass, G. (Ed.) **Evaluation Studies Review Annual: Volume 1.** Beverly Hills: Sage, 1976. Guttentag, M. (Ed.) **Evaluation Studies Review Annual: Volume 2.** Beverly Hills: Sage, 1977.

3, See the following articles in this volume: Edwin Fenton's for "Civic Education," Marcus Lieberman's for "Reasoning Ability," and Clark Power's for "Building Community."

4. The Alverno faculty's definition of the "valuing ability" is detailed in Earley, M., Mentkowski, M., and Schafer, J. **Valuing at Alverno: The Valuing Process in Liberal Education.** Milwaukee, Wisconsin: Alverno Productions, 1980.

5. For a description of each of these abilities, see the following book: Alverno College Faculty. **Liberal Learning at Alverno College.** Milwaukee, Wisconsin: Alverno Productions, 1976.

6. The five-year process by which Alverno redefined liberal education in terms of student abilities and reshaped its curriculum accordingly is reviewed in detail in **Liberal Learning at Alverno College,** 1976.

7. How the faculty define, teach for, and assess these levels is explicitly detailed in Earley, M., Mentkowski, M., and Schafer, J. **Valuing at Alverno: The Valuing Process in Liberal Education.** Milwaukee, Wisconsin: Alverno Productions, 1980.

8. Members of the Valuing Competence Division whose work is reported in this paper are: P. Burns, M. Earley, R. Hufker, P. Hutchings, A. Huston, E. Kisinger, G. Kramer, M. Mentkowski, and J. Schafer. They represent eight different disciplines or professional areas.

9. These criteria are available from the Valuing Competence Division, Alverno College, 3401 South 39th Street, Milwaukee, Wisconsin 53215.

10. The term "illuminative evaluation" is borrowed from M. Parlett and D. Hamilton (see References).

11. The assessment process is described in a recent book: Alverno College Faculty. **Assessment at Alverno College.** Milwaukee, Wisconsin: Alverno Productions, 1979.

12. Sample instruments are available from the Valuing Competence Division.

13. The complete instrument is available from the Valuing Competence Division.

14. These objectives, and the student profile study described in the next section are funded by the National Institute of Education. See Mentkowski, M., and Doherty, A. **Careering after College: Establishing the Validity of the Abilities Learned in College for Later Success** (NIE-G-77-0058) Milwaukee, Wisconsin, Alverno College, 1977. Progress reports submitted to NIE from the Office of Evaluation detailing progress toward completing this three-year grant are available from the Office of Evaluation, Alverno College, 3401 South 39th Street, Milwaukee, Wisconsin 53215.

15. The instruments listed are available as follows:

Test of Cognitive Development: John Renner, School of Education, University of Oklahoma.

Sentence Completion Test: In Loevinger, J., and Wessler, R. **Measuring Ego Development.** Vol. 1. San Francisco: Jossey-Bass, 1970.

Moral Judgment Instrument: L. Kohlberg, Center for Moral Education, Harvard University.

Defining Issues Test: James Rest, 330 Burton Hall, University of Minnesota.

Measure of Vocational, Educational and Personal Issues. L. Knefelkamp, College of Education, University of Maryland.

16. The following instruments are available from McBer and Company, 137 Newbury Street, Boston, Massachusetts 02116:

Learning Style Inventory

Picture Story Exercise

Analysis of Argument

Test of Thematic Analysis

Life History Exercise

The Adaptive Style Inventory is available from David Kolb, Department of Organizational Behavior, Case Western Reserve University.

Watson-Glaser Test of Critical Thinking is available from Harcourt, Brace and World.

17. See Lois Erickson's article, this volume.

REFERENCES

Alverno College Faculty. **Faculty Handbook on Learning and Assessment**. Milwaukee, Wisconsin: Alverno Productions, 1977.

Alverno College Nursing Faculty. **Nursing Education at Alverno College**. Milwaukee, Wisconsin: Alverno Productions, 1979.

Colby, A. "Evolution of a Moral-Developmental Theory." *New Directions for Child Development*, 1978, 2, 89-104.

Doherty, A., Mentkowski, M., & Conrad, K. "Toward a Theory of Undergraduate Experiential Learning." *New Directions for Experiential Learning*, 1978, 1, 23-35.

Earley, M., Mentkowski, M., and Schafer, J. **Valuing at Alverno: The Valuing Process in Liberal Education**. Milwaukee, Wisconsin: Alverno Productions, 1980.

Friedman, M., & Mentkowski, M. "Instrument Validation in a Competence-Based Curriculum: An Empirical Illustration." Paper presented at the meeting of the American Educational Research Association, Boston, April 1980.

Geertz, C. **The Interpretation of Cultures**. New York: Basic Books, Inc., 1973.

Gilligan, C., & Murphy, J. M. "From Adolescence to Adulthood: The Moral Dilemmas of Reconciliation to Reality." *Moral Education Forum*, 1979, 4(4), 3-13.

House, E. R. "Justice in Evaluation," In G. V. Glass (Ed.), **Evaluation Studies Review Annual** (Vol. 1). Berverly Hills: Sage Publications, 1976.

Kohlberg, L. "Moral Stages and Moralization: The Cognitive-Developmental Approach." In T. Lickona (Ed.), **Moral Development and Behavior: Theory, Research and Social Issues.** New York: Holt, Rinehart & Winston, 1976.

Kohlberg, L., Colby, A., Gibbs, J., & Speicher-Dubin, B. "Standard Form Scoring Manual." Unpublished manuscript, Harvard University, 1978.

Loevinger, J. & Wessler, R. **Measuring Ego Development.** Vol. 1. San Francisco: Jossey-Bass, 1970.

McClelland, D. "Testing for Competence Rather Than for 'Intelligence'." *American Psychologist*, 1973, 28, 1-14.

Mentkowski, M. "How Does a Psychologist Resolve Moral Dilemmas When Conducting Research?" In J. B. Richmond (Chair), Moral Issues in Conducting Research with Children. Symposium presented at the biennial meeting of the Society for Research in Child Development, New Orleans, 1977.

Mentkowski, M., & Much, N. **Alverno College Student Perspectives Interview.** Milwaukee, Wisconsin: Alverno Productions, 1980.

Mosher, R. "Theory and Practice: A New E.R.A.?" *Theory Into Practice, 16*(2), 81-88.

Parlett, M., & Hamilton, D. "Evaluation as Illumination: A New Approach to the Study of Innovatory Programs." In G. V. Glass (Ed.), **Evaluation Studies Review Annual** (Vol. 1). Beverly Hills: Sage Publications, 1976.

Perry, W. **Forms of Intellectual and Ethical Development in the College Years: A Scheme.** New York: Holt, Rinehart, & Winston, 1968.

Piaget, J. "Intellectual Development from Adolescence to Adulthood." *Human Development*, 1972, 15, 1-12.

Power, C., & Reimer, J. "Moral Atmosphere: An Educational Bridge Between Moral Judgment and Action." *New Directions for Child Development*, 1978, 2, 105-116.

Rest, J. R. "New Approaches in the Assessment of Moral Judgment." In T. Lickona (Ed.), Moral Development and Behavior: Theory, Research and Social Issues. New York: Holt, Rinehart & Winston, 1976.

Rest, J. R. The Impact of Higher Education on Moral Judgment Development (Technical Report # 5). Minneapolis: University of Minnesota, Minnesota Moral Research Projects, September, 1979.

Scriven, M. "Evaluation Bias and Its Control." In G. V. Glass (Ed.), Evaluation Studies Review Annual (Vol. 1). Beverly Hills: Sage Publications, 1976.

Chapter 4

EVALUATION OF CHARACTER DEVELOPMENT
IN AN UNDERGRADUATE RESIDENTIAL COMMUNITY

John M. Whiteley

The focus of this chapter is on evaluation of character development in an undergraduate residential community. The intent is to describe the problems such an undertaking presents, and how the staff of the Sierra Project approached solving those problems. Prior to addressing the evaluation questions, it is necessary to describe the Sierra Project.

The Sierra Project is designed to facilitate and study dimensions of character development in college students. As a research project, the Sierra endeavor was to study the developmental status of college freshmen, and to assess the growth and development of those freshmen over the course of their undergraduate experience on such dimensions as moral reasoning, ego development, and sex role choices. As a curriculum development project, the goal of Sierra was to construct a replicable curriculum intended to facilitate the transition from high school to college life, stimulate psychological development from late adolescence to early adulthood, foster a consideration of future lifestyle choices and career decisions, and challenge the learner to apply his or her educational experiences to problems in the broader community through community service. A detailed description of the project and its research component is provided by Whiteley (1980a) and Whiteley (in press). The curriculum is described by Whiteley and Loxley (1980) and Loxley and Whiteley (in press).

SIERRA PROJECT APPROACH TO EVALUATION:
INTRODUCTION

The Sierra Project approach to evaluation was multi-faceted, reflecting the complex nature of the project and the fact that there are no specific developmentally oriented instruments that expressly measure the broad concept of character development. Important constructs within the concept of character development such as a psychological sense of community, moral reasoning, sex roles, and ego development have approaches to measurement which are all in process of development, refinement, and/or basic modification. Further, since the Sierra Project is a naturalistic intervention, it occurs with voluntary participants in a college residence hall as one component of the freshman year experience at the University of California, Irvine. In such a setting there are practical limitations of how much testing is either possible or desirable.

There were a number of basic questions the approach to evaluation was intended to address:

Did the intervention produce changes and did those changes endure?

What parts of the intervention, under what conditions, produced what identifiable developmental changes?

Who benefited most from the intervention with the particular population of students?

What experiences were the most impactful, particularly on students' thinking about moral decisions?

Each of the above basic questions were approached with quite different evaluation techniques. The next sections of the paper present each of those different techniques, and the questions each is intended to address.

EVALUATION AND DURATION OF CHANGES:
THE SURVEY DESIGN

The question of whether the intervention produced changes and whether those changes endured was approached with a longitudinal survey design. Students were tested at the beginning and end of their freshman year, then at the end of their sophomore, junior, and senior years. The survey design consisted of measurements of:

MORAL REASONING:

Kohlberg Moral Judgment Interview
(Kohlberg, 1973)

Rest Opinions About Social Problems Test
(Rest, 1973, 1979)

EGO DEVELOPMENT

Loevinger Sentence Completion Test for Measuring Ego Development
(Loevinger, 1966; Loevinger and Wessler, 1970)

SEX ROLE CHOICES

Bem Sex Role Inventory
(Bem, 1974; Bem, 1975)

PSYCHOLOGICAL SENSE OF COMMUNITY

Environmental Assessment Inventory
(Stokols, 1975)

LOCUS OF CONTROL

Rotter I-E Scale
(Rotter, 1966)

PARTICIPANT INFORMATION

Background Questionnaire
(Whitla, 1977)

STUDENT EXPERIENCE AT COLLEGE

College Experience Questionnaire
(Whitla, 1977)

The Survey Design, through the use of these instruments, is an evaluation approach to studying the impact of the curriculum experience, the developmental status of freshmen, and the longitudinal development of moral reasoning in college students. When repeated test administrations occur over the course of four years of undergraduate study, the Survey

Design allows an assessment of whether changes in the freshman year persist over time.

There are several important choices to be made in the Survey Design approach to evaluation: consideration of cohort differences from year to year, choice of statistical technique, and choice of a control population.

Cohort differences become an important variable to address in the context of the distinction between developmental change versus developmental differences (Huston-Stein and Baltes, 1976). Simply stated, students in one freshman class may differ markedly from students in another freshman class. In order to make certain that developmental changes are accurately assessed, it is necessary to recognize that the socio-cultural experiences of one group of late adolescents may differ markedly from another. The alternate turmoil and quietude on campuses over the past decade, in the context of the childhood and adolescent experiences that preceded college enrollment for each class of students, did produce differences that must be taken into account in the evaluation design if developmental change patterns are to be a focus. For that reason we included the collection of extensive background and college experience data.

Choice of statistical technique is an important evaluation decision in a survey design. We have chosen to present the results of a repeated-measures analysis of variance. This statistical technique presents the effects of group membership (control vs. experimental) and sex as well as the effect of change over time (pre-post in the freshman year, as well as sophomore, junior and senior year test administrations).

The choice of a control population is a critical decision, particularly in the context of a longitudinal, naturalistic study. The question which must be addressed is how representative the final sample is of the population as a whole. With a longitudinal investigation, the sample may be reduced by attrition to a point where the remaining subjects do not reflect the population from which they were originally drawn. Freshmen as a group tend to experience a particularly high level of attrition in a research-oriented public university.

In the freshman year, the control groups allow us to study the effects of the curriculum on the experimental group. Over the course of the four years, the control groups allow us to examine persistence of change from the freshman year, as well as the development of students over the course of the undergraduate experience. We chose two control groups in the freshman year. One control group wanted the Sierra experience, but were randomly assigned to another residence hall. The other control group was a "collateral control group." Collateral control groups allow a scrutiny of "the effects of experimental attrition—to determine in what manner the sample deviates from its original representative nature at subsequent measurement points" (Schaie, 1973, p. 255). Collateral control groups are selected randomly from the class as a whole, with the group used in each subsequent test administration different for each of the four years. In other words, any individual student who once participates in a collateral control group is excluded from any further participation.

EFFECTS OF COMPONENTS
OF THE INTERVENTION

In order to investigate the question of what parts of the intervention under what conditions produced what changes, we used both a Topical Design and an Intensive Design. The Topical Design centered on an evaluation of the effects of each curriculum module. Data were collected before and after specific modules of the curriculum were presented. The assertion training module, for example, was evaluated by student reports and by the College Self-Expression Scale (Galassi, Delo, Galassi & Bastien, 1974; Galassi & Galassi, 1974). The GAIT Empathy Scale (Goodman, 1972), the Carkhuff Empathy Scale (Carkhuff, 1969), and the Carkhuff Gross Dating of Facilitative Functioning (Carkhuff, 1969) were used to evaluate the empathy training.

EVALUATING INDIVIDUAL VARIATION
IN RESPONSE TO THE INTERVENTION

As with the Topical Design, the Intensive Design as an evaluation approach applies only to the experimental population and not the control groups. In the Intensive Design, the focus is on each individual as a case study with data collection continuous throughout the year. For the classes of 1980 and 1981, major sources of data were student journals, sophomore staff journals, and staff reports.

Although there were several case studies undertaken by staff members for the classes of 1980 and 1981, a rigorous application of the Intensive Design was made only with the class of 1982. There were two reasons for this decision. The first reason was the unavailability in the first two years of the project of staff with the necessary skills to conduct the intensive evaluation properly. The second reason was that the regular staff of the project was fully extended to implement the other components of evaluation and curriculum, and did not have the time to acquire the skills to conduct the investigation.

A detailed report of the Intensive Design with the class of 1982 is provided by Resnikoff and Jennings (in press). The basic question they addressed was, "Under what conditions have what kinds of students changed in what specific ways?" They investigated the various impacts of the university environment upon students with the methodology structured to gain a phenomenological view of students' thoughts, feelings, and behavior over the course of the year.

Seven students out of a total of 17 who volunteered for the Intensive Design were chosen at random, by sex, for this study. They were interviewed initially every week for the first month of school and then on an every other week basis for the remainder of the academic year. Interviews were of a semi-structured nature. Students were asked to report thoughts. feelings and behaviors from the previous two weeks. Incidents which remained in students' minds were presumed to be of importance. The two researchers (Resnikoff and

Jennings) alternated interviewing the same students in order to provide a reliability check on researcher perceptions. In addition, data from a number of different sources were gathered. The curriculum coordinator kept detailed notes of class events; dorm staff were requested to provide observations on events which were occurring. Interview notes were dictated following each interview. Students kept detailed journals of their activities, often writing their interpretations of, or reflections on, their experiences.

In studying the results from the nine months of Intensive Design data collection, the various pieces of data were reviewed and then divided into two major categories. The first category focused upon those events, and reactions to those events, which were common across the Sierra class experience. One example would be where individuals may have reported some similar reactions to a common impactful stimulus. Another example would be where students employed certain similar behaviors to resolve conflicts among themselves in the latter part of the year in a manner which had not been present earlier in the year. In this latter case, connecting the new behaviors to specific instructional experiences or events was somewhat more difficult.

A second category of outcomes are unique student experiences. This category can best be summarized as changes in individuals, not common across the entire sample, but traceable to the beliefs, values, and personal styles of these individuals, and the interaction of those characteristics with environmental pressures.

The Intensive Design approach applied by Resnikoff and Jennings (in press) provided a perspective on the changes occurring in students, and related those changes to events during the year. Some of those events had been provided by the formal structured Sierra curriculum, but many had to do with non-curricular sources of influence. Other important sources of change which we would not otherwise have been able to consider without this evaluation approach were:

1. The social structure of the dormitory

2. The physical structure of the dormitory

3. The impact of the Irvine campus in both academic and social relations

4. The particular developmental stage at which an individual may view him/herself

5. The particular pressures of leaving home for the first time

6. Testing one's adequacy, academically, socially, and sexually

7. Certain other individual differences which each one of these students brought to the study.

The Survey and Topical Designs do not have the capability which the Intensive Design has of connecting components of the intervention with outcomes over a long time frame, in this case the length of the freshman year. Additionally, the approach used by Resnikoff and Jennings (in press) allows the explanation of individual variations in outcome, and the generation of new theoretical insights and hypotheses for further exploration and systematic testing.

IDENTIFYING CHARACTERISTICS
OF THOSE WHO CHANGE THE MOST

The evaluation approach taken by Magana (1979) addressed the question of who benefited the most from the intervention with our particular population of students. Multidimensional scaling and hierarchical cluster analysis were used to differentiate among individuals in the Sierra sample she studied. The developmental measures from the Survey Design included the level of moral reasoning, ego development, locus of control, self esteem, alienation, sex-role identification, and attitudes toward people served as the data source.

Her first task was to determine whether meaningful patterns of individual differences existed in the sample. If patterns of differences were found to exist, her second task was to discover whether there were significant differences in the rate and nature of change for students with different initial types of profiles.

The basis of the Magana (1979) approach is to divide students according to the similarities in their initial testing. The clusters of students so identified are then examined at subsequent testings to see if there are differences in the extent and type of change which occurred between testings. Change is considered from two perspectives. The first is quantitative, where the researcher looks for intercluster differences in change on each of the measures in the profile. The second is qualitative, where the task is to see if there are any changes in the overall pattern of the profile.

IDENTIFYING IMPACTFUL EXPERIENCES: PERCEPTIONS OF THE PARTICIPANTS

The final approach to evaluation utilized in the Sierra Project was to focus directly on student perceptions of what had most impacted their thinking about moral decisions. The previously described Topical and Intensive Designs had provided some sources of data on what experiences occurred during the freshman year which had particularly notable impact upon the participants in the intervention.

The evaluation approach chosen to investigate what students saw as having most impacted their thinking about moral decisions was a modification of **The Moral Reasoning Experience Check List**, a structured interview developed by Volker (1979). The approach was to directly ask students what had been impactful experiences for them, and what had been important contributing influences to their thinking about moral issues. Once the students gave an answer, the interviewer would follow up systematically to learn more about the details of the experience, what about it had contributed to their thinking, and how they thought differently now, in their opinion, as a result of the experience.

The modified **Moral Reasoning Experience Check List** has been administered to a small sample from the class of 1979, which served as the pilot group for the Sierra Project. The administration was at the end of their senior year. The task presented to them was to reflect back on their freshman year experiences. With the class of 1983, students will be asked at the end of their freshman year what experiences had been most impactful for them. In addition, they are being pretested and post-tested on the Rest **Opinions About Social Problems Test** (Rest, 1979) and the **Socio-Moral Reflection Measure** (Gibbs, Widaman, and Colby, 1980). This will allow us to evaluate whether there is any relationship between level of moral reasoning, type of experience perceived as impactful, and amount of change in moral reasoning during the freshman year.

REFLECTIONS ON THE SIERRA APPROACH TO EVALUATING CHARACTER

The definitional nature of character development, the state of the current approaches to measurement available for evaluation, the research goals, the curriculum development goals, the voluntary status of participants, the skills of the staff, and the naturalistic setting for the Sierra Project all contributed to the form which the evaluation has ultimately taken.

We have learned much the hard way, particularly during the exploration years with the class of 1979. I had three early fantasies about the project basic to the evaluation. The first fantasy was that no one would sign up for it. This turned out not to be the case. The second fantasy was that no one would choose to participate in the post-test evaluation after a year of work had been invested. This turned out not to be the case. The third fantasy was that the control groups would end up changing more than the experimental group. On some dimensions this turned out to be quite true.

Had we been limited to only several of our approaches to evaluation, we would have been missing important data necessary to address central questions, and to understand in some detail what students were experiencing, and how they were changing. A basic strength of this approach to evaluation is that important aspects of the complexity of the Sierra Project could be captured and analyzed. Each of our different sources of data collection and analysis served to provide quite valuable perspectives on the process of character development and what influences it during the college years.

REFERENCES

Bem, S. "The Measurement of Psychological Androgyny." *Journal of Consulting and Clinical Psychology*, 1974, 42, 155-162.

Bem, S. "Sex-Role Adaptability: One Consequence of Psychological Androgyny." *Journal of Personality and Social Psychology*, 1975, 31, 634-643.

Carkhuff, R. R. **Helping and Human Relations** (Vol. I & II). New York: Holt, Rinehart & Winston, 1969.

Galassi, J. P., Delo, J. S., Galassi, M. D. & Bastien, S. "The College Self-Expression Scale: A Measure of Assertiveness." *Behavior Therapy*, 1974, 5, 165-171.

Galassi, J. P. & Galassi, M D. "Validity of a Measure of Assertiveness." *Journal of Counseling Psychology*, 1974, 21, 248-250.

Gibbs, J. C., Widaman, K. F. & Colby, A. "The Socio-Moral Reflection Measure." In L. Kuhmerker et al. (Eds.), **Evaluating Moral Development and Evaluating Educational Programs That Have a Value Dimension**. Schenectady, NY: Character Research Press, 1980.

Goodman, G. **Companionship Therapy: Studies in Structured Intimacy**. San Francisco: Jossey-Bass, 1972.

Huston-Stein, A. & Baltes, P. "Theory and Method in Life-Span Developmental Psychology: Implications for Child Development." In Reese, H. W. (Ed.), **Advances in Child Development and Behavior** (Vol. II). New York: Academic Press, 1976.

Kohlberg, L. "Standard Scoring Manual." Unpublished manuscript, Harvard University, 1973.

Loevinger, J. "The Meaning and Measurement of Ego Development." *American Psychologist*, 1966, 21, 195-206.

Loevinger, J. & Wessler, R. **Measuring Ego Development**. San Francisco: Jossey-Bass, 1970.

Loxley, J. C. & Whiteley, J. M. **Character Development in College Students** (Vol. II). Schenectady, NY: Character Research Press, in press.

Magana, H. A. "Individual Differences in Multiple Assessment and Their Relationship to Rate of Development: Implications for Developmental Research and Intervention." Unpublished doctoral dissertation, University of California, Irvine, 1979.

Resnikoff, A. & Jennings, S. "Influences on Freshmen: Intensive Case Study Design." In J. M. Whiteley, Character Development in College Students (Vol. I). Schenectady, NY: Character Research Press, in press.

Rest, J. "The Hierarchical Nature of Moral Judgment: A Study of Patterns of Comprehension and Preferences of Moral Stages." Journal of Personality, 1973, 41(1), 86-109.

Rest, J. Development in Judging Moral Issues. Minneapolis: University of Minnesota Press, 1979.

Rotter, J. "Generalized Expectancies for Internal Versus External Control of Reinforcement." Psychological Monographs: General and Applied, 1966, 80(1, Whole No. 609).

Schaie, K. "Methodological Problems in Descriptive Developmental Research on Adulthood and Aging." In J. R. Nesselroade and H. W. Reese (Eds.), Life-Span Developmental Psychology: Methodological Issues. New York: Academic Press, 1973.

Stokols, D. "Toward a Psychological Theory of Alienation." Psychological Review, 1975, 82(1), 26-44.

Volker, J. "The Moral Reasoning Experience Check List." Unpublished manuscript, 1979.

Whiteley, J. M. "A Developmental Intervention in Higher Education." In V. L. Erickson & J. M Whiteley (Eds.), Developmental Counseling and Teaching. Monterey, CA: Brooks/Cole, in press.

Whiteley, J. M. Character Development in College Students (Vol. I). Schenectady, NY: Character Research Press, in press.

Whiteley, J. M. & Loxley, J. C. "A Curriculum for the Development of Character and Community in College Students." In V. L. Erickson & J. M. Whiteley (Eds.), Developmental Counseling and Teaching. Monterey, CA: Brooks/Cole, 1980.

Whitla, D. Value Added: Measuring the Outcomes of Undergraduate Education. Cambridge, MA: Harvard University Office of Instructional Research and Evaluation, 1977.

Chapter 5

THE DEVELOPMENT AND SCORING OF LAWRENCE KOHLBERG'S MORAL JUDGMENT INSTRUMENT

Lisa Kuhmerker

This chapter is abstracted from a monograph by the author published in 1978.[1] The source for the guidelines for structural interviewing and scoring is the Scoring Manual used at the 1977-1979 Scoring Workshops at the Center for Moral Education.[2]

The sequencing of modes of reasoning about moral dilemmas has represented the study of half a lifetime for Lawrence Kohlberg. The refinement of a methodology for the measurement of this sequential development has been a strenuous and frustrating task both for Kohlberg and his co-workers and for the philosophers, psychologists and practitioners who have tried to understand and apply his techniques.

Kohlberg discovered structure and sequence in the way human beings approach real and hypothetical dilemmas. His staging of sequential levels of moral reasoning linked moral development research to the theory and research of John Dewey and Jean Piaget. It showed that moral development, like all learning, depended on interaction between the organism and the environment. It showed that moral learning was not a matter of social imitation, but that each person constructed and reconstructed his/her view of the world; that the cognition of one phase of a person's life experience became "re-cognized" with each emerging level of maturity.

These powerful ideas have given a tremendous stimulus to researchers in all aspects of social reasoning and behavior.

Just as Freud's place in the field of psychoanalysis is assured whether or not many of his ideas have been discarded or transformed by subsequent research, so Kohlberg's place as "the father of modern moral development theory" is assured whether or not his stage theory becomes modified in the future, and whether or not a new generation of researchers find better (and simpler) ways of tuning in to the structure of people's reasoning and behavior.

The refinement of methodology for the measurement of moral development is the primary means through which Kohlberg has validated his theory of stage and sequence in the development of moral judgment. He offers three research instruments for this purpose: a standard moral interview format, a standard-form scoring system, and "structural" interviewing techniques.

THE DEVELOPMENT OF SCORING SYSTEMS

The "Standard Scoring System," also identifiable as the "Concern Scoring System," is the third structural method for the analysis of the moral judgment interview that has been developed by Kohlberg and his staff at the Center for Moral Education.

The earlierst method, the "Ideal Type Rating" published in 1958, combined the use of story scoring and sentence scoring. It was based on equating the content of responses and attitudes toward each of the dilemmas, and looking at the patterns of responses within each stage as if it were an ideal type or composite photograph.

When Kohlberg applied this method to the scoring of longitudinal cases, he found a number of deviations from the notion of invarient sequence. In his doctoral dissertation in 1968, Richard Kramer (Harvard University) analyzed a good deal of the longitudinal material Kohlberg had collected and found quite a number of anomalies in sequence. Kohlberg had begun to anticipate that this would happen and thought it was, in part, a result of faults in the scoring method.

This led Kohlberg and his associates to make two basic

changes: first, they did some redefining of the stages at a structural level. Second, the rating was also more structural. That is, the rater did not orient so much to the content. The method systematically tried to control for content by scoring in terms of each of the ten moral issues, but left it to the rater to pool material from a number of stories on a given issue.

The second stage of development in the scoring technique (1972) analyzed response units that were smaller than the story of the moral dilemma, but larger than single sentences. This "Structural Issue Rating" method yielded stage consistent responses, but the descriptions of typical stage-specific responses in the manual were very general. Scorers could not match the responses they elicited to specific statements in the manual. Thus, the system took a year or more to learn and it was still difficult for independent scorers to reach agreement. Students of this historical development of structural issue rating may order "A Handbook for Assessing Moral Reasoning" by N. Porter and N. Taylor.[3]

The "Standard Scoring System" limits itself to the scoring of two issues per dilemma. Thus the Heinz Dilemma, for example, is now scored only on the issues of life and law. The question of whether or not Heinz should be punished if he steals the drug has been made into a separate story, whose two issues are law and punishment.

The new scoring system takes cognizance of subsidiary issues within a story. In the Heinz story, for example, the love of the husband for the wife (affiliation) is a concern. But in the actual scoring, the subsidiary issue of affiliation is scored with the "life issue."

While the new scoring system limits itself to two issues per story, it makes a new and sharp distinction between issues and concerns. Responses to the Heinz story can serve as examples. A subject might say, "he should save his wife and maybe later she'll save him." The issue in this case is "life," the concern is "positive reciprocity." If a subject were to say "he shouldn't steal the drug because he'll get punished" the issue again would be "life," but this time combined with "concern for sanctions."

The content of the moral interviews has undergone relatively little change in the last twenty years. Kohlberg invented dilemmas that pose hypothetical conflict situations in which the subject must make one of two choices. (For example, in the Heinz dilemma, Heinz must either steal a drug to save his wife's life, or obey the law). The interview question is phrased so that the subject must coordinate and weigh the importance of one set of values (such as life) in relation to another set of values (such as law) and apply these values to a specific situation.

Kohlberg still uses many of the dilemmas he posed to subjects in the 1950s. Changes and additions in the dilemmas selected for interview have had a triple purpose: (a) sharpening of the need for choice between two, and only two, alternative values; (b) selecting dilemmas that represent moral conflicts about which pre-adolescents, adolescents, and adults are concerned in every culture; (c) selecting dilemmas that tap issues that are significant to persons at the higher levels of moral development.

It is the "structure" behind the content that has absorbed the attention of Kohlberg and his associates. What instrument, what scoring technique, will measure moral reasoning most effectively? How can the teaching of "structural" interviewing techniques become more standardized and simplified? And, finally, as the issues, norms, and elements are classified most accurately, what dimensions of moral reasoning, concern and commitment are screened out by this selective process?

STRUCTURAL INTERVIEWING

What is the purpose of structural interviewing? It is to penetrate beyond a subject's opinions, attitudes, or beliefs, to the reasoning or justification which directs them. Good or "structural" interviewing means fulfilling the need to:

1. explain to the subject the interview goal of trying to understand and bring out his or her underlying thinking on moral dilemmas;

2. ascertain that the subject fully understands a given dilemma before proceeding with questions on it;

3. encourage the subject to answer prescriptively rather than descriptively ("Do you think Heinz *should* steal the drug?");

4. enable the subject to reflect on his moral suppositions through probing ("What do you mean by justice?"[4]).

What characterizes a good dilemma? The first requirement is that the dilemma has an important issue, favoring a "pro" and a "con" action choice (e.g., in the Heinz dilemma the issue of life leads to a "pro" choice and the issue of law to a "con" choice in the matter of stealing a drug). In standardizing dilemmas and probe questions and constructing parallel forms, there is deliberate focus on two issues even when a third must be de-emphasized.

> "This separation of content into two units per story is somewhat arbitrary, however, since in reality each side of the choice involves for most subjects a cluster of values or issues. In order to reflect this and still maintain the basic two issue organization, the scoring system recognizes minor or subsidiary issues, which tend to cluster with the standard issues on opposing sides of the dilemma conflict.

> "In order to reflect the fact that the two standard issues in a dilemma actually consist of a cluster of value concerns, a further classification by content is provided by the system of moral *norms*. Thus, the full set of values used by the subject are called the moral norms. The two or more moral values or value clusters defining the polar choice in a dilemma are called the issues ... The choice or general value being supported is the issue, the *values* brought to bear on that choice (property, authority, contract) are norms."[6]

> "A second difference between values as issue and values as norms is that norms are values 'in' the person, something (s)he 'carries around with her/him' that defines or

conceptualizes, for her/him, the basis of the values of objects or situations. Issues, on the other hand, involve something external or 'out there,' which are valued social objects, institutions, or events rather than internal values and norms of individuals. The 'externality' of the moral issues is indicated by the fact that they can be conceptualized as moral institutions and are pre-established as relevant for a subject by the nature of the moral dilemma to be resolved. That is, the moral issues in an interview are chosen by the experimenter who writes the dilemma. In any given response, the choice of which norm is brought to bear on the issue is to a large extent a function of the particular respondent's values and beliefs."[7]

ISSUES, NORMS, AND ELEMENTS

How globally—vs. how differentially—should one analyze subjects' moral thinking? The strategy of Kohlberg, Candee, Colby and Gibbs is to start very globally in the approach to the interview data and *then* become more refined. In practical terms this means that at the beginning of each dilemma, the subject is required to make a choice.

"This choice between issues is what the subject is most essentially *doing* in his thinking, and constitutes the most basic line of cleavage, our first functional division: *between issues.* We start our analysis, then, by differentiating and grouping together the responses addressed to one or the other issue for the dilemma. If we were to stop here and try to begin our scoring, however, we would be trying to operate at a level which is still too global. The subject's reasoning on each issue is not one homogeneous mass, and so is not usable as a reliable scoring unit. Within the issue material we must identify particular values or objects of concern. As we said, when we use values in this way, we refer to them not as issues but instead as *norms*. For example, a subject who judges that Heinz should steal the drug may have as his object of concern the value of a human life (life norm). The life norm is not the only possible object of concern, however, and this is why we must be a bit more refined in our value classification. Considering again the Heinz-dilemma example, the subject's thinking on the life issue may focus not on the life norm but instead on the value of someone one loves (affiliation norm), the value of obeying one's conscience (morality norm), or on the recognition that a person misuses his discovery (property norm). So within the response material falling under a given issue, we further differentiate and group together certain component *norms* (on the life issue in the Heinz dilemma, the subject may evidence only one norm in his thinking, or as many as four)."[8]

To put it another way, in supporting an issue, the subject brings norms, such as property, authority or contract, to bear on that choice. Issues involve something external or 'out there,' that is values as a social institution or event, but the norms that are brought to bear on the issues are largely a function of the values and beliefs in the subject. A subject must choose between two issues (law or life), but need not choose either love or life, love or contract as norms, because norms are always, in some sense, terminal values.

In practice, norm groups are still too gross to serve as effective scoring units. What are the particular concerns or considerations for which the norms serve as objects? For example:

"A person who in the Heinz dilemma has 'chosen' the life issue and focuses on the affiliation norm must do so in some specifiable way. Let us suppose his judgment is that Heinz should steal the drug for his wife because Heinz married her and should love and care about her. Beyond identifying the life issue and affiliation norm, we can specify a consideration of duty or obligation (*since* he married her, he should . . .; Heinz's marriage implies a duty); we say then that the 'duty' element (element) is brought to bear or operates upon the affiliation norm in this case."[9]

The particular concerns or considerations, the thoughts that become a recurrent theme or leitmotif in many protocols are labeled "elements" of the scoring system.

> "The norms are cognitively describable independent of the subject's value attitude toward them, the elements are not. Norms are categories of cognition as well as of valuing. We can ask, 'What do you or does society mean by property, or law, why have property?' without assuming to the subject a valuing attitude toward property. We can assume that the subject has a cognitive or descriptive or value-neutral concept of law, somewhat independent of a 'lawfulness' attitude. When we ask what is 'equity' or 'justice,' we want a definition of the subject's idea of a *justice principle*, not his description of a social institution.

> "Norms are terminal values in relation to issues but are still in some sense instrumental values. *Elements* are *terminal* in relation to norms. When we ask, 'Why value law or property?' we are treating them as values instrumental to some more terminal value. These moral terminal values are the elements or principles. We can value law in terms of a more terminal value, social welfare, or equity-justice. 'Welfare' or 'justice' as moral elements, attitudes, or principles are not institutions. The Department of Welfare is not the welfare principle. A principle or attitude gives value to an institution or norm, but is not itself a social norm or role. We can also value one of the value objects or norms as instrumental to another, i.e., we value law to preserve life. But norms are not fully terminal, we can always ask, 'Why value life?' and get to welfare (happiness) or justice (human rights).

> "Elements are internalized psychological value dispositions, norms need not be. Elements are general across situations and types of action, norms are not. *Property* or *life* is a value in some dilemmas, not in others. Welfare is a value in any situation. The norms, then define kinds

of action, law breaking and life saving, in kinds of situation, the elements do not. The elements are more life motives, the welfare element is the 'motive' of altruism, the negative reciprocity element is the 'motive' of revenge, the prescriptive role-taking element is the 'motive' of empathy.

"The elements, then are more abstract and general than the norms. The elements are unitary and abstract, the norms are concrete complexes of attitudes. 'Lawfullness' as a norm involves a complex of attitudes which differ according to whether they involve a concern for social welfare, for justice or equity, for conscience, or for fear of punishment, etc.

"The elements do not define a choice conflict (unless a common norm or issue to which both apply is first specified); the issue or norm values do. Usually, elements are too abstract to define a conflict unless a norm/issue value is first specified. The values of life and law can conflict. 'Should we save life or obey the law?' Without specifying or holding norm constant, elements do not define conflicts. 'Should we save life or serve human welfare?' No conflict. 'Should we obey the law or serve human welfare?' No conflict. If we hold norm constant, we can use elements as issues. 'Should we save the most lives (welfare) or hold each life of equal value (justice)?' That is Dilemma 5, the Captain's dilemma. Our dilemmas, however, are typically internorm conflicts, not inter-element conflicts. Probe questions about the central issue are also typically norm-oriented, not element-oriented. Most probes are, 'If you should steal to save the life of your wife, should you also do it for a stranger, or if you don't *love* her?' (The norm of life vs. affiliation.[10])"

SUBSTAGES

Within each stage there are qualitative differences in subject response that warrant the subdivision of stages into A and B substages. While both substages have the same social perspective, judgments at substage are more equilibriated and reversible than their A counterparts. Central to all the B elements is the fairness orientation, a definition of rights in terms of what the self would expect in the role of the other, or in terms of the ideal of what should be expected.

Not only does Substage B make reciprocal the considerations at Substage A, but considerations at Substage B of a lower stage often become formalized at A of the next higher stage. For example, the idea that an individual's affection for a loved one can generalize to all human beings (hence, an individual can "have a relationship" with all human beings) is first developed at Stage 3.

WOULD IT BE AS RIGHT TO STEAL IT FOR A STRANGER AS FOR HIS WIFE?

Yes, a life is like love. *You can love people who are not even close to you*, strangers as well as those close to you. To give life is beautiful, to save a life is the same. (Stage: 3B; Issue: life; autonomy.)

However, what was an extended feeling of affect at Stage 3B, becomes a codified value that should be recognized by law and society at Stage 4A:

SHOULD THE DOCTOR GIVE THE WOMAN THE DRUG THAT WOULD MAKE HER DIE SOONER?

The doctor should not give her the drug because it is always wrong to take a life. Human life is the highest value we have. It is sacred. (Stage: 4A, Issue: life/having a right.[11])

Grouped under Substage B are all the elements of fairness orientation that affirm the individual's autonomy and uniqueness. The other orientation which constitues the B Substage is Mode C, the Idealizing and Perfectionistic Mode. The key concepts here are that right actions are those which lead to the improvement or uplifting of the actor's own personality or are those which foster improvement in the quality of relations between groups of individuals.

THE MORAL JUDGMENT INSTRUMENT
AS A RESEARCH TOOL

It is helpful to think of the Moral Judgment Instrument as a research tool for the validation of moral development theory and the measurement of stage change in individual subjects, rather than as an evaluation strategy for measuring effects of education in large-scale projects. No one should try to score the MJI without a training course and/or careful study of the Moral Judgment Scoring Manual. Doctoral students may wish to avail themselves of the option of having their protocols professionally scored by staff at the Center for Moral Education.

REFERENCE NOTES

1. Kuhmerker, Lisa. **Developments in Kohlberg's Theory and Scoring of Moral Dilemmas.** Occasional Paper No. 6. Philadelphia, PA: Research for Better Schools, Winter 1978.

2. Colby, Anne, Gibbs, John C., Speicher-Dubin, Betsy, Power, Clark C. and Candee, Dan. **Assessing Moral Stages: A Manual.** (Preliminary edition available from Center for Moral Education, Harvard University Graduate School of Education, Cambridge, MA 02138.)

3. Porter, Nancy & Taylor, N. "A Handbook for Assessing Moral Reasoning." (Unpublished manuscript, 1972. Available from Center for Moral Education.)

4. **Assessing Moral Stages: A Manual** (see reference above) pp. 2-3.

5. Ibid, p. 9.

6. Ibid, pp. 9-10.

7. Ibid, p. 11.

8. Ibid, pp. 15-16.

9. Ibid, p. 16.

10. Ibid, pp. 20-21.

11. Ibid, p. 24.

Chapter 6

DIALOG: LAWRENCE KOHLBERG TALKS TO LISA KUHMERKER ABOUT MORAL DEVELOPMENT AND THE MEASUREMENT OF MORAL JUDGMENT

Lisa Kuhmerker: *The completion of the Standard Scoring Manual is a milestone in your career and a fitting time to ask you to share your ideas and plans with researchers and practitioners in moral education.*

Larry Kohlberg: With the Standardized Scoring Manual and its validation on the longitudinal data we have completed a task that has taken over twenty years, which is to define structural moral stages and to demonstrate their existence empirically as something culturally universal. In the meantime, one important use of these concepts and methods has been to assess educational change.

In the last five or six years I've begun to look at moral education not simply in terms of what stages in moral reasoning have to say about it, but in terms of all the goals and processes that are involved in moral education. I am now concerned with taking up issues of content as well as structure. I'm interested in dealing with moral action as well as moral reasoning. I am also concerned with dealing with social environments in a more adequate way; dealing with the moral atmosphere or moral climate of institutions.

Where did the basic questions, hypotheses and research strategies that shaped your doctoral dissertation on moral development come from?

87

They came from reading Piaget's clear developmental orientation in **The Moral Judgment of the Child**. I was also influenced by George Herbert Mead and James Mark Baldwin, who had lucid, philosophically constructed stages of moral development.

Piaget posed pairs of hypothetical dilemmas to young children. As far as you know, had anyone else thought to develop a systematic way to elicit thinking about hypothetical dilemmas?

Other people had used hypothetical dilemmas but not in a way that made it possible to elaborate the reasoning and structure underlying them. For example Frank Sharf, a professor of philosophy at the University of Wisconsin, questioned college students about moral dilemmas to find out if everyone was really a utilitarian at heart and related all judgments to consequences. I used variations of some of his dilemmas in my dissertation. Other people have used hypothetical dilemmas as well, though without a developmental framework.

Did you do a pilot study before you began your actual dissertation?

You might call it that. I lived near a grocery store. Sometimes I would catch kids who were coming in to buy some groceries and pose them some quick dilemmas—so I actually had fairly extensive pre-testing.

What were the hypotheses on which you based your dissertation?

At the time, I assumed that Piaget had outlined the basic dimensions for the development of moral judgment and I intended to use his stages even though I was working with a somewhat older group of kids. The original hypothesis also assumed that social class and social perspective were significant antecedents of development, an idea I took from Herbert Mead. I also used measures of parent identification, which I though would relate to moral judgment development. Once I actually started interviewing kids I found that Piaget's system didn't really capture what was going on developmentally, nor did any other a priori system. So I tried to develop a more adequate sort of stage theory.

Did you actually rate responses in terms of stages at that time?

I didn't call them stages at that time; I called them developmental types. I identified six developmental types on three major levels; pre-conventional, conventional and post-conventional.

So from the beginning you saw that children had distinct, sequential ways of meaning-making?

I was aware of sequence and hypothesized that there would be such a sequence, but I knew that without longditudinal data I could not demonstrate the existence of stages. The data I used went somewhat beyond age trends. I looked at the patterns of correlations, via the Guttman Simplex, to research the developmental order of the types of moral thought.

Basically, would it be correct to say that the definition of stages one to four has not given you many problems or complications?

The stages that have stayed pretty well intact are Stages 1 and 2, and to a lesser extent Stage 3. But the more advanced the stage, the more redefinitions have evolved. Some of the things we originally called Stage 4 we now call Stage 3. We also went through a phase of stage redefinition following our findings of what appeared to be regression in the college years, when students seemed to be moving from a Stage 5 to a Stage 2. This led us to revised definitions of Stages 4, 5 and 6.

You've interviewed many adolescents who were moving into and through Stages 3 and 4. How do you think the larger social setting influences development beyond Stage 3? For instance, in what way have some of our national crises affected the development of young people?

That's probably very difficult to say. It seemed to me that the way conflicts were perceived by college students in the Sixties was condusive to moral development past Stage 4. This is very impressionistic, but it seems to me that there are fewer Stage 5 college students now than there were in the Sixties. Today's students are likely to be Stage 4 in some relativistic sense, but in their questioning of conventional morality we see much more privatism among students, rather than a move toward reform through radical, principled solutions.

Does it surprise you that principled thinking is so rare?

No, that isn't surprising to me. In every society that we've studied the majority of adults are at Stage 4 or 3/4. Principled thinking demands a certain degree of freedom of movement—as Erickson might term it—a chance to explore without having to make premature commitments. Conflict is another factor that can spur development from conventional to principled thinking.

The college climate is condusive for the experiencing of both of these conditions.

In our longditudinal sample all those who reached Stage 5 did go to college and some had graduate education as well. I think of the college years as a time for reflection. A moratorium away from premature commitment.

In making the leap from theory to educational intervention how did you come to select moral discussions and the Just Community approach as your primary educational intervention strategies?

The moral discussion approach was stimulated by Moshe Blatt's finding that after a semester of discussions one third of the students moved up one stage as compared to a control group which did not change in the same period. The notion of cognitive conflict and exposure to the next stage led us to test the use of hypothetical dilemmas further, with rather consistent, positive results. That is why many schools have incorporated hypothetical dilemmas into their curriculum from the elementary through the high school level.

Why do some youngsters make a dramatic transition from one stage to another while others seem reasonably unaffected?

Well, there is a readiness factor that's highly accounted for by the Piagetian cognitive stage and partly by the social perspective taking level (a la Selman). For instance, Clarence Walker in Canada took a group of Stage 2 children and tested them for formal operations and social perspective-taking capacities. Then he exposed them to a short series of discussions in which the child had to ask two adults for advice, and was given a pro answer by one and a con answer by the other. With this very minimal amount of stimulation he found that a very large proportion of the subjects who had the logical and social perspective-taking pre-requisites moved from Stage 3 to 4. None of the Kids without the capacity for formal operations or perspective-taking showed any movement from 2 to 3. This can account for a lot of the movement we have found in Blatt's and other studies.

A hypothetical dilemma is generally designed so that students have to choose between two-and only two-values. Real-life dilemmas aren't usually so clearcut.

I've always been fairly sympathetic to the criticism of the sole use of the hypothetical dilemma approach.

How did this lead you to the Just Community approach?

If you're going to deal with real dilemmas in school then you're dealing with a hidden curriculum as well as with an academic one. That means in particular that the teacher's authority and the authority system of the school is in some question. If you're going to discuss real dilemmas in school you have to be willing to let some kind of decision come out of the discussion. Once teachers and administrators are prepared to allow a process of democratic decision making to come out of the discussion of real dilemmas, you have a Just Community School.

Are you beginning to have a sense of how positive intervention stimulates the moral atmosphere of the school?

Clark Power's dissertation was an effort to show that conscious effort to raise the moral atmosphere of the school through the Just Community approach embraced by the teachers and consultants and myself *did* lead to a movement from a Stage 2 to a 3-4 moral atmosphere with a higher phase of shared norms of community.

Do you have either data or hypotheses about how sensitivity to the moral atmosphere of the school affects students out of school and in new school settings?

We haven't researched this and I don't think we have solved the problem of how to help students bridge the gap . . . . students who go to college after being in a Just Community School come back and tell us that they miss the sense of community they had in High School.

In addition to the line of research you are probing with the interviews on the moral atmosphere of the school, what else do you think researchers and practitioners should be evaluating in programs that have a value dimension?

I've sometimes recommended a test that samples a broader band of value dimension than the MJI and still is developmental, and that is useful for assessing educational change in a values program that does not focus explicitly on the development of a sense of justice: The Loevinger Test of Ego Development.

How about an instrument for measuring moral sensitivity?

Our own approach predefines the dilemmas as moral dilemmas involving justice and rights. Another way would be to take dilemmas which might not be perceived as moral dilemmas and see whether some people were sensitive to the dilemma aspect of them. This comes a little closer to the approach of Carol Gilligan who asks subjects to define their own dilemmas.

Disregarding for the moment the differences in complexity of administration and scoring between the Moral Judgment Instrument and the Defining Issues Test, or John Gibbs' Socio Moral Reflection Measure, how can a program evaluator decide which instrument to use?

Recognition tests like James Rest's or John Gibbs' and the Moral Judgment Instrument were developed for somewhat different purposes. The purpose of the MJI is to classify the subject by stage—or by a mixture of two stages—and to be able to then trace change or progress in this qualitative way from one stage to the next. The evidence that we have accumulated on the Harvard test really justifies that you can fairly validly assign individuals to a single stage by the interview method. If, on the other hand, all you want is a general picture of whether or not your class as a whole is more advanced after the educational intervention than at the beginning, you can do that as well with the DIT as with the MJI.

So the DIT shows movement along a continuum and the MJI focuses on stage change. What if we want to measure the moral atmosphere of the class or school as a whole in terms of stage change?

We've taken a long time and have made very slow progress in developing an assessment of the moral atmosphere of the school. We don't yet have anything that is nearly as standardized and reliable and valid as the MJI. The basic tool we use to define moral atmosphere consists of a series of school dilemmas which are first asked as hypothetical dilemmas. When we follow up by asking students if such a dilemma actually occured in their schools, how do they think people *would* act, and how do they think people *should* act, we are trying to get at shared or collective expectations and norms as well as the individual's own moral judgments. We probe for information about shared and collective norms and expectations around issues like property, trust, helping and so forth and classify these by stage and then by phase, which probes the extent to which students feel that common expectations can be enforced. In our study of the early years of the Cluster School we found more rapid growth in the moral atmosphere of the class than in the individual stage change of students.

If a school made no effort to stimulate student interaction and moral development would you expect the moral atmosphere of the school to change over a period of years?

Well the kids are growing older, so you would expect some individual stage change and this would lead to some development of shared expectations even without teachers or administrators attempting to consciously create a higher level moral atmosphere.

You have mentioned an interest in returning again to a study of "content" as well as "structure." Supposing you had a subject at Stage 2 who was still Stage 2 when you re-interviewed him some years later. Would you expect the content of the Stage 2 response to be very consistent for the same subject after a period of years or would he reflect the intervening life experiences even if the structure of his thinking had not changed? I imagine you have a good deal of longitudinal data that can help to answer this question.

That's a good question which we haven't studied yet in our longitudinal data. I think we will find that a subject will move from an A-Substage to a B-Substage as a result of development during a passage of time even if there hasn't been a change in the major stage. The person would probably go from a 2-A to a more egalitarian 2-B point of view. Substages are a little complicated to elaborate, but essentially they are defined by the criterion judgments. A-Substage criterion judgments refer to utilitarian consequences, to following rules for their own sakes. B-Substage judgments make some explicit reference to fairness or balance or role-taking. That is to say, the B-Substages are more universalized and prescriptive than the A-Substages.

Our interview today will be published some months before the publication of the final version of your Scoring Manual. Researchers who are eagerly awaiting the statistics on the validity and reliability of Standard Form Scoring will appreciate your offer to let us print several tables with important reliability data in this volume. Would you summarize for us why you believe that the data confirms the validity and reliability of your stage theory?

Before you can establish much about the validity of an instrument you have to know its reliability. Our test-retest figures are especially important because they give us the estimate of measurement error that is most relevant to our longitudinal data. As shown in Table 1, correlations between Time 1 and Time 2 for Forms A and B, are both in the high 90's. Since the correlation could be very high without much absolute agreement between scores at Time 1 and Time 2, we have also presented percent agreement figures. For almost all subjects, the scores of Time 1 and Time 2 were within one-third of a stage of each other. If we look at global scores based on a nine-point scale—the five stages and the four transition points between stages—we find between 70 and 80% complete agreement.

RELIABILITY OF STANDARD FORM SCORING

Table 1

Test-retest Reliability

Correlation T_1 - T_2: Form A: .96 (Rater 1); .99 (Rater 2)

Form B: .97 (Rater 2)

Percent agreement within one-third stage: Form A 93%

Form B 94%

Form A & B 100%

Percent agreement using pure stage and mixed stage scores
(9 categories: 1, 1/2, 2, 2/3, 3, 3/4, 4, 4/5, 5)

Form A (N=43)	70% (Rater 1), 77% (Rater 2)
Form B (N=31)	75% (Rater 2)
Forms A & B (N=10)	80% (Rater 2)

Percent agreement using major/minor stage differentiations
(13 categories: 1, 1(2), 2(1), 2, 2(3), 3(2), 3, 3(4),
4(3), 4, 4(5), 5(4), 5)

Form A	59% (Rater 1), 70% (Rater 2)
Form B	62% (Rater 2)
Form A & B	70% (Rater 2)

Almost all subjects received scores within one-third stage of each other on two interviews conducted about a month apart. About three quarters received identical scores on the two interviews when a nine-point scale is used, and between one-half and two-thirds received identical scores with the most finely differentiated thirteen-point scale.

Test-retest interviews described above were also used for assessing inter-rater reliability. The figures for inter-rater reliability (Table 2) look roughly comperable to the test-retest figures—almost all interviews were scored within a third of a stage of each other by any two raters, and on about half to two-thirds of the interviews the two raters assigned identical scores even when using the thirteen category system. The correlation between raters 1 and 2 was .98.

RELIABILITY OF STANDARD FORM SCORING

Table 2

Inter-Rater Reliability

Correlation - Raters 1 and 2, Form A test-retest interviews = .98 percent agreement:

		Within 1/3 Stage	Complete Agreement (9 categ.)	Complete Agreement (13 categ.)
Form A Rater Pair	1	100	88	53
	2	100	88	63
	3	100	75	63
	4	88	88	63
	5	88	88	63
Form B Rater Pair	6	100	78	78

Alternate form data are based on those test-retest subjects who received both forms A and B on the 233 longitudinal interviews which include both forms. A single rater scored independently both forms of the test-retest sample interviews. Percent agreement between Forms A and B for this sample were comparable to test-retest and inter-rater reliability: 100% of the interviews were given scores within one-third stage of each other for the two forms, 75% received identical scores for Form A and B using the nine-point scale, and 67% received identical scores for the two forms using the thirteen-point scale. The correlation between moral maturity scores for Forms A and B in this sample was .95.

The level of agreement across forms for the longitudinal data is not as high (see Table 3). This is to be expected since Form A was scored by rater 1 and Form B by rater 2. That is, the reliability figures confound form and rater differences.

Table 3

Alternate Form Reliability

Longitudinal Sample (N=193)

    Correlation Form A - Form B = .84
        (Rater 1 for Form A, Rater 2 for Form B)

    85% Agreement within 1/2 Stage
        (other percent agreement figures not yet available)

Test-retest Sample (Rater 2 for both forms)

    Correlation Form A - Form B = .95

    Percent Agreement (9 categories) = 75%

    Percent Agreement (13 categories) = 67%

    Percent within 1/3 Stage = 100%

Now turn to validity: The basic test of validity for the Standard Scoring System of the MJI is the extent to which blind scoring of the longitudinal data conforms to the criteria of invarient sequence without stage skipping. We found that Form A and B of the MJI combined, only 1% of the subjects showed backward movement. That is, with forty subjects tested four times there were 171 possibilities for moving either up or down but only two subjects showed any downward stage movement. This is even far less downward movement than the 10% test-retest figures. There were no cases of stage skipping. In the three to four year interval between the testing of longitudinal subjects not one person moved more than one-third stage upward. It is rather remarkable how this method of interviewing and scoring captures and confirms the theory of sequential stage development.

The additional component of the construct validity of the stage test is the notion that the individual should score fairly consistently at one stage, or at the most, at two stages. Since most of our subjects were still developing, we would expect them to both be in a predominant stage and moving toward the next stage. We find, in fact, that over two-thirds of a subject's thinking—around 70%—is at one stage with the rest of the responses recorded at the adjacent stage. A mere 2% of the subjects had scores distributed across three stages.

These are all characteristics of the idea of a stage construct that should be met by the tester, and to a large extent our data shows that these criteria have been met. At the end of twenty years of work I believe we can state that the Moral Judgment Instrument is well within the limits of acceptable reliability and validity.

Chapter 7

THE SOCIO MORAL REFLECTION MEASURE

John C. Gibbs, Keith F. Widaman and Anne Colby

There is a widespread need in the field of socio moral development and education for a readily usable production-task instrument. To date, the only available standard research instrument which permits a direct (i.e., production-task) assessment of moral reasoning is that developed by Kohlberg and colleagues (Colby, Gibbs, Kohlberg, Speicher-Dubin, Power, and Candee[1]). The Kohlberg instrument (henceforth represented as the MJI, Moral Judgment Instrument) has recently been found to be psychometrically acceptable (Colby, Kohlberg, and Gibbs;[2] Kohlberg, Colby, and Gibbs;[3] Kohlberg[4]), but requires a considerable investment of time and money for its effective use with most subject populations. Generally, valid and reliable use of the MJI requires the individual interviewing of subjects by experienced interviewers, and the scoring of the protocols by specially trained scorers. Typed manuscripts from taped interviews are also often required.

Perhaps partly because of the hurdle imposed by workshop training and personnel (interviewer, transcription) demands, a number of alternative moral judgment tests which do not make such demands have appeared in the literature. These tests (e.g., by Bloom, 1977; Hogan, 1970; Maitland and Goldman, 1974; Page and Bode, 1978; Rest et al, 1974; Swegan and Rodgers[5]) are all based on recognition tasks of one sort or another. The most prominent of these tests,

Rest's Defining Issues Test (DIT), requires subjects simply to evaluate the relative importance of Kohlbergian-stage-significant considerations pertaining to the solution of Kohlberg-type moral dilemmas. Differential patterns among subjects' comparative rankings of the considerations then permit distinctions among subject performances along a developmental scale. Since the DIT requires only quantitative assessments of already-provided concepts (and hence draws only recognition and evaluation processes), its use offers clear logistical advantages over the MJI. Individual interviewing is unnecessary and protocol assessment can even be done by computer. On the other hand, the DIT leaves the researcher interested in socio-moral reasoning with at best only an indirect index of that variable. As Rest himself (1975) notes, "The Defining Issues Test was not designed simply to be an easier way of assessing moral judgment than Kohlberg's test" (p. 748). Rather, the DIT was designed to provide an assessment tool for studying the developmental ability to discriminate and appreciate socio-moral and political arguments. Such an ability can be considered to be a functional aspect of moral judgment, and therefore in these terms the DIT provides a direct assessment instrument. Nonetheless, the researcher who seeks to study the moral reasoning or reflection aspect of moral judgment through use of the DIT will find that s/he is able to say little about moral reasoning per se at the conclusion of the study.

The proposed new instrument, the Socio Moral Reflection Measure (SRM), would offer to researchers the best of both (production and recognition) worlds: it would enable researchers to tap reflective moral judgment directly from subjects' self-produced socio moral justifications, yet would make only modest logistical demands (since it is designed for group administration and straightforward protocol assessment). The SRM uses the Kohlberg dilemmas as a means for eliciting in questionnaire format subjects' written justifications of their evaluations regarding certain cited normative values (e.g., evaluations of the importance of saving a life, obeying the law, or keeping a promise). In general, establishment of a standardized and construct-validated SRM would make an important methodological contribution to research in moral and social development.

It will be helpful for understanding the departure represented by the SRM to discuss the general features of the moral judgment interview format. These features can be elucidated through consideration of the probe questions actually used for one of the dilemmas, the famous Heinz dilemma. Following the action-choice questions ("Should Heinz steal the drug? Why?") are the following standard probe questions (elaborated upon by individual interviewers):

2. If Heinz doesn't love his wife, should he steal the drug for her?

2A. Why or why not?

3. Suppose the person dying is not his wife but a stranger (and the stranger can get no one else to help). Should Heinz steal the drug for the stranger?

3A. Why or why not?

4. If you favor stealing the drug for a stranger: suppose it's a pet animal he loves. Should Heinz steal to save the pet animal?

4A. Why or why not?

5. Is it important for people to do everything they can to save another's life?

5A. Why or why not?

6. It's against the law for Heinz to steal. Does that make it morally wrong?

6A. Why or why not?

7. Should people do everything they can to obey the law?

7A. Why or why not?

7B. How does this apply to what Heinz should do?

These standard probes represent those interview questions which have been found, over the past two decades, to be most efficacious in eliciting structurally significant response material.

There would seem to be two general functions served by these probe questions (as well as by the probe questions used for the other dilemmas); both of these functions in turn serve the broader objective of promoting the structural scorability of the interview data. First, some of the questions serve to insure the thought-provoking power of the dilemma by modifying, elaborating upon, or highlighting circumstances of the dilemma so that the dilemma may become more problematic for the individual subject. For example, the subject who without much thought decides that Heinz should steal the drug may find the choice less straightforward if it is assumed that Heinz doesn't love his wife (Question 2) or if stealing the drug is for a stranger (Question 3) or a pet (Question 4). Accordingly, the justifications for action choices may become more thoughtful—and usually more structurally valid—in response to the "why" sequels for these questions (Questions 2A, 3A, 4A). Similarly, Question 6 explicitly highlights one of the features of the dilemma (the fact that stealing the drug would be against the law) and challenges the subject to deal with its implications. Such variations or challenges also help the scorer to identify the particular line of justification which is the most fundamental for a given subject. Finally, such questions promote the structural yield from a given subject's responses since the questions often prompt a subject to provide alternative justifications; for example, a subject whose fundamental concern is with Heinz's motivating love for his wife will have to think anew if it is specified that Heinz does not love his wife (Questions 2, 2A).

The remaining questions seem to serve a second function, namely, that of broadening the frame of reference for the subject's discourse beyond the single instance or specific action choice to the level of general prescriptive practices or normative values such as saving a life (Question 5) or obeying the law (Question 7). Some subjects will spontaneously justify their prescriptive action choice on the practice or normative-value level anyway; but for the many subjects who do not, these questions are helpful. And again, just as structural scorability is enhanced where a subject must justify a more difficult decision (first function), it is also enhanced where a subject must broaden that justification to explicitly address a general normative value (second function). Also important is the fact that these general normative questions serve to alleviate the complexity of the scorer's classification task: they insure that the response material for at least certain questions will be codable by the norm explicitly cited in the question (e.g., "life" in Question 5, "law" in Question 7).

The rationale behind the SRM is this: might not a simplifying systematization of the best features of the MJI make possible a more practicable production-task instrument? If varying the dilemma circumstances has been found to promote subjects' thoughtfulness, then why not make circumstantial variation a consistent and comprehensive, rather than just a partial, feature of the question format? If asking directly for justifications of the importance of otherwise only implied normative values has also been found to reduce classification difficulties and to promote the depth—and hence scorability—of subjects' responses, then why not ask such questions for all of the norms entailed? Indeed, it is possible to combine the two features for each question. One can vary (or at least highlight) each major normative circumstance of each dilemma and then, for each such variation, ask for the subject's justification of the norm involved. By combining on each question the best features of the MJI, we gain the prospect of a research instrument which, although allowing the subject slightly less latitude for free response, greatly reduces through its systematic structure the classification and assessment demands upon the protocol scorer. Moreover, the improved efficacy of such a format for eliciting structurally scorable responses from the subject enhances the feasibility of group administration of the task; group administration may become feasible not just for some, but for *most* subject populations.

These ideas behind the SRM can be illustrated with the Heinz dilemma. The first question, "What should Heinz do? Steal/don't steal/can't decide (circle one)? Why?" is considered to be simply a warm-up question, tentatively included because it was found to help the subject orient to the dilemma and to the production of justifications. The subject then reads these instructions: "Let's change things about the problem and see if you still have the opinion you circled above (should steal, should not steal, or can't decide). Also, we want to find out about the things you think are important in problems like these, especially *why* you think those things are important."

The questions which follow (specifically, the "B" parts) are termed *norm stems*. They probe in a systematic fashion for subjects' justifications of the respective importance of the normative values entailed in the dilemma:

1.   What if Heinz doesn't love his wife? Should Heinz: steal/not steal/can't decide (circle one)?

1A. How important is it for a husband to steal to save his wife, even if he doesn't love her? very important/ important/not important (circle one).

1B. *Why is that very important/important/not important (whichever one you circled)?*

2.   What if the person dying isn't Heinz's wife but instead is a friend (and the friend can get no one else to help)? Should Heinz: steal/not steal/can't decide (circle one)?

2A. How important is it to do everything one can, even break the law, to save the life of a friend? Very important/important/not important (circle one).

2B. *Why is that very important/important/not important (whichever one you circled)?*

3A. What about for a stranger? How important is it to do everything one can, even break the law, to save the life of a stranger? Very important/important/not important (circle one).

3B. *Why is that very important/important/not important*
     (whichever one you circled)?

4.   What if the druggist just wants Heinz to pay what the
     drug costs to make, and Heinz can't even pay that?
     Should Heinz: steal/not steal/can't decide (circle one)?

4A. How important is to for people not to take things
     that belong to other people? Very important/impor-
     tant/not important (circle one).

4B. *Why is that very important/important/not important*
     (whichever one you circled)?

5A. How important is it for people to obey the law? Very
     important/important/not important (circle one).

5B. *Why is that very important/important/not important*
     (whichever one you circled)?

The standard arrangement for these questions is threefold.
The "what if" starters for the basic questions negate or highlight one of the circumstantial values of the dilemma and ask
the subject to decide anew, given this variation, whether
Heinz should steal the drug (a "can't decide" choice is per-
mitted). The "A" component of each question then asks for
an evaluation of the importance of the general normative
practice or value implied by the particular "what if" variation.
It is the "B" component, asking as it does for the subject's
justification of the evaluation given in "A," which becomes
the focus of attention for the scorer. As noted, we call these
aspects of the questions the *norm stems*. Questions 1B and
2B probe for various aspects of the affiliation norm, and
Questions 4B and 5B probe for aspects of the law-and-prop-
erty norms. Question 3B covers the life norm. The norm
stems are deliberately intermingled, and secondary reference
to opposing values often deliberately included, in order to
preserve the richness of the dilemma situation as a context
for the subject's responses. Nonetheless, each "B" question,
or norm stem, renders explicit some aspect of a particular
normative value in the dilemma and requires a direct justification of the value. Of course, subjects typically refer, in re-

sponding to the norm stem, to the concrete dilemma circumstances as specified in the earlier parts of the question. This is also deliberate, since we agree with Lawton and Hooper (1978) that such "concrete props" are crucial for facilitating reflective judgment.

It can be seen that this format is designed to maximize the advantages which can be discerned—but which are used only partially—in the MJI questions. The changes are evident. Not just for some of the questions, but for *all* of the questions, subjects' justifications must relate to thought-provoking variations in the dilemma. Not just for some of the questions, but for *all* of the questions, subjects' justifications must deal directly with a general normative value entailed in the dilemma situation. The SRM is also designed for efficient and simplified scoring: no justification data are elicited from the subject until the subject has been positioned into the structurally richest level of reflection, and until a particular normative feature of the dilemma has been framed.

Pilot research on the SRM has been carried out at the University of Massachusetts in Boston, where undergraduates have served both as subjects and as data collectors. This pilot research has been invaluable for refinement of the SRM questionnaire format, for the preliminary organization of a scoring procedure, for the beginning construction of an assessment manual, and for an assessment of the SRM's concurrent validity. The first author conducted this work while a part-time professor at the University of Massachusetts, with the assistance of Dr. Marvin Berkowitz, Dr. William Jennings, Garot Blake, and Wilma Blocker. Especially notable is the assistance from Berkowitz, who engaged his University of Massachusetts students in an exercise of pairing the SRM with the MJI for the purpose of assessing concurrent validity. Twenty-seven members of Berkowitz's class served as investigators with a data collection assignment. The student investigators received interviewing skills preparation by Berkowitz. Each investigator collected two pairs of protocols, one pair from a subject in the 9-15 year old range, and one pair from the same-sex subject in the 15-24 year old range. Each subject received either the MJI (through oral interviewing, with subject responses probed and recorded verbatim by the investigator), followed immediately by the SRM (completed in writing by the subject), or received the two tests in reverse sequence. Crossed with order of administration was type of form: each subject received either the MJI Form A and the SRM Form B, or the MJI Form B and the SRM Form A (same-form administration was not feasible because of the high content overlap between the corresponding forms of the tests). In this fashion, 55 MJI and 55 SRM protocols (25 MJI Form B/SRM Form A, 30 MJI Form A/SRM Form B) were collected from 55 students. Mean age of the subjects was 16.6 years. Thirty-one of the subjects were female. Order of administration was evenly balanced by sex and age. Two Ohio State University graduate students, the second author and Mark Kernan (both of whom participated in the June 1979 Kohlberg Moral Judgment Scoring Workshop), scored the MJI protocols. The principal investigator independently scored the SRM protocols by norm stem on an impressionistic basis. The Pearson product-moment correlation between the MJI and the SRM was .85; with age partialled out, the correlation was .50 ($t = 3.92$, $df = 52$, $p < .001$; see McNemar, 1955, p. 185). Exact global agreement between the two tests was 38% and agreement within a minor stage was 83.6%.

Our current aims, in the order in which they are being pursued and accomplished, are as follows. With the assistance of a grant from the National Institute of Mental Health, we will:

1. construct an SRM assessment manual;

2. develop SRM scoring procedures and computational algorithms;

3. assess concurrent construct validity for the SRM;

4. establish reliabilities on the SRM;

5. develop annotated training materials;

6. assess construct validity for the SRM; and

7. finalize the SRM assessment manual, questionnaire format, scoring procedure, and computational algorithms.

In general, Brown and Herrnstein (1975) note, the topic of moral reasoning represents "a very substantial aspect of human psychology" (p. 307). There is currently a widespread need in this area for a readily usable production-task measure. The SRM is designed to fill this need, since it could be group administered and relatively easily scored. Thus, the SRM could play a major role in facilitating research in a wide variety of research areas bearing on socio moral reasoning, such as moral education, delinquency, correctional programs, judgment-action relationships, and socialization.

REFERENCE NOTES

1. Colby, A., Gibbs, J. C., Kohlberg, L., Speicher-Dubin, B., Power, C. and Candee, D. **Assessing Moral Stages: A Manual.** Book in preparation. (Preliminary edition available from Center for Moral Development and Education, Harvard University Graduate School of Education, Cambridge, MA 02138.)

2. Colby, A., Kohlberg, L. and Gibbs, J. C., "A Longitudinal Study of Moral Judgment." Paper presented at the meeting of the Society for Research in Child Development, San Francisco, April, 1979.

3. Kohlberg, L., Colby, A. and Gibbs, J. C., "The Measurement of Stages of Moral Judgment." Unpublished manuscript, Harvard University, March, 1979.

4. Kohlberg, L., "The Meaning and Measurement of Moral Development." In B. Kaplan (Ed.), **1979 Heinz Werner Memorial Lectures,** in press.

5. Swegan, R., and Rodgers, R. **An Objective Test of Moral Judgment.** Work in progress, The Ohio State University, 1979.

REFERENCES

Bloom, A. H., "Two Dimensions of Moral Reasoning: Social Principledness and Social Humanism in Cross-Cultural Perspective." *Journal of Social Psychology,* 1977, **101**, 29-44.

Brown, R. and Herrnstein, R. J. **Psychology**. Boston: Little, Brown and Company, 1975.

Hogan, R. "A Dimension of Moral Judgment." *Journal of Clinical Counseling Psychology,* 1970, **35**, 205-212.

Lawton, J. T. and Hooper, F. H. "Piagetian Theory and Early Childhood Education: A Critical Analysis." In L. S. Siegel and C. J. Brainard (Eds.), **Alternatives to Piaget: Critical Essays on the Theory**. New York: Academic Press, 1978.

Maitland, K. A. and Goldman, J. R. "Moral Judgment as a Function of Peer Group Interaction." *Journal of Personality and Social Psychology,* 1974, **30**, 699-704.

McNemar, Q. **Psychological Statistics** (4th Ed.). New York: John Wiley and Sons, Inc., 1955.

Page, R. and Bode, J. "An Objective Assessment of Moral Reasoning." *Moral Education Forum,* 1978, Nov., 14-15.

Rest, J. R. "Longitudinal Study of the Defining Issues Test of Moral Judgment: A Strategy for Analyzing Development Change." *Developmental Psychology,* 1975, 738-748.

Rest, J. R., Cooper, D. Coder, R., Masanz, J. and Anderson, D. "Judging the Important Issues in Moral Dilemmas—An Objective Measure of Development." *Developmental Psychology,* 1974, **10**, 491-501.

Chapter 8

THE DEFINING ISSUES TEST:
A SURVEY OF RESEARCH RESULTS

James R. Rest

The Defining Issues Test ("DIT") is a multiple-choice, objectively scored measure of moral judgment. It can be administered to large groups of subjects at the same time and can be scored by computer. The rationale for the test is essentially derived from Kohlberg's theory of moral judgment; however, the DIT is not simply an objective test version of Kohlberg's test. Because it involves a task which assesses a somewhat different aspect of moral judgment, it defines the stages somewhat differently, and it has involved different research strategies. Furthermore, the DIT cannot be used with young subjects (lower than the reading level of the average 12-year-old), as can Kohlberg's test. Nevertheless, the DIT has interested many researchers not only because of its ease of administration and scoring, but also because of the substantial data base now accumulated on the test which supports its reliability and validity.

The DIT assumes that people at different developmental stages perceive moral dilemmas differently—particularly in what they see as the crux of a moral problem and in what considerations they regard as the most important ones. The DIT is concerned with how people define the issues in a moral dilemma. Presumably if people are presented with different statements about the crucial issue of a moral dilemma, people at different developmental stages will choose different statements as representing the most important issue.

The DIT uses six moral dilemmas, three of which were taken from Kohlberg's Interview, and three from Lockwood's dissertation (1970). These dilemmas were chosen because extensive interviewing had already shown what kinds of things people spontaneously say in response to these dilemmas. The DIT dilemmas include the familiar story about Heinz and the drug. (Heinz's wife is dying of cancer and a druggist in town has a drug that might save her; however, the druggist demands an exorbitant price for the drug and Heinz cannot raise the money; should Heinz steal the drug?) After a subject reads a dilemma, twelve issue-statements are listed. The subject is asked to read each one and indicate on a 5-point rating scale how important each issue-statement is in making a decision about what ought to be done in the dilemma. For instance, regarding the Heinz dilemma, the subject first reads the issue, "Whether a community's laws are going to be upheld." If the subject thinks that this issue is the crux of the dilemma and of great importance in deciding what Heinz ought to do, then the subject is instructed to rate that item high. If the item has some relevance but is not decisive in and of itself, then the subject is instructed to give the item a medium rating. If the item is ridiculous, is irrelevant, or doesn't make sense, then the item is to be rated low. Other items for the Hienz dilemma include: "Isn't it only natural for a loving husband to care so much for his wife that he'd steal?" "Is Heinz willing to risk getting shot as a burglar or going to jail for the chance that stealing the drug might help?" "What values are going to be the basis for governing how people act toward each other?" These four items were designed to represent the way that the crucial issue might be conceived from a Stage 4, Stage 3, Stage 2 and Stage 6 point of view, respectively. Twelve items in all are presented to subjects for each of the six dilemmas, producing ratings on 72 items. After *rating* the items, subjects are asked to *rank* the four most important items from each set of twelve.

A variety of scores can be derived from this kind of rating and ranking data. One of the most useful scores has been the "P" index: The relative importance that a subject gives to

Stage 5 and 6 items ("principled" considerations), using weighted ranking data. Davison (in Rest, 1979) has recently developed a scaling technique which yields an overall composite index of development, the "D" index, based on weighted rating data. Scores for Stages 2, 3, and 4 can also be derived from subjects' questionnaires, although the reliability of these scales is not as high as the "P" and "D" indices. (See Rest, **Revised Manual**, 1979, for scoring details and technical data on various scales.) A detailed discussion of the theoretical rationale of the DIT and technical design features is contained in another recent book (Rest, 1979). There, a number of technical issues are discussed: the number of items written for each stage, item order, continuous indexing versus stage typing indices, relation of decision data to item evaluation, architecture of stage definitions in DIT research versus the recent Kohlberg scheme, etc.

As with every method of assessment, there are advantages and disadvantages to the DIT's method. The three most serious threats to the internal and external validity of a test like the DIT are (1) that subjects may randomly check off responses without even reading the items, dilemmas and instructions; (2) subjects may pick out items that seem complex and sophisticated, even when they do not understand their meaning; (3) subjects may try to fake high on a recognition task since they don't have to discuss or justify their answers. Special features were built into the DIT to deal with these problems. For random checking, a "Consistency Check" between the rating and ranking is used to identify subjects who are putting check marks down in a meaningless pattern. If a questionnaire does not pass the "Consistency Check" it is discarded from further analysis. Similarly, in order to identify subjects who are picking items on the basis of their apparent complexity rather than on their meaning, the DIT contains a number of "M" items—that is, items written to sound impressive and sophisticated but which don't mean anything (e.g., "Whether the essence of living is more encompassing than the termination of dying, socially and individually"). If a subject selects too many of these "M" items, his questionnaire is also discarded. Thirdly, several studies have been conducted to determine if subjects can fake high without invalidating their questionnaire on the M score. It seems subjects cannot fake high although they can fake low (see Rest, 1979, Chapter 7).

Several hundred studies have now been completed on the DIT involving over 10,000 subjects, and cannot be summarized very adequately here. Rest (1979), contains an extensive summary and interpretation of results. Nevertheless some idea of this research might be conveyed by the following list of findings:

1. Cross-sectional samples of junior high students, senior high students, college students and graduate students show strong age-educational trends. The variance accounted for by age-education reaches 50% in some studies. Junior Highs average in the 20s on the P index, senior highs in the 30s, college students in the 40s, and graduate students in the 50s. Moral philosophy and political science doctoral students score highest, in the 60s.

2. In longitudinal studies, subjects show significant upward change both in terms of group averages and in terms of upward shifts in individual scores. Time-sequential and cohort-sequential analyses show that these changes cannot be attributed to cohort or generational effects. Testing effects and sample-bias are not serious problems, either.

3. The DIT correlates in the .60s in several studies with moral comprehension, and correlates significantly with a variety of measures of cognitive development (Piaget's Formal Operations, Perry's Intellectual and Ethical Development, Cornell Critical Thinking Test, etc.), and generally in the .20 to .40 range with measures of IQ, aptitude and achievement.

4. The DIT correlates in the .60s and .70s in several studies with Kohlberg's test although lower in homogeneous samples.

5. The DIT correlates in the .60s in several studies with people's stances on controversial political-moral issues.

6. Test-retest stability over several weeks averages .81 in a number of samples; internal consistency averages .78.

7. In longitudinal studies, increases in DIT scores are accompanied by increases in Comprehension and in shifts in socio-political attitudes (lower scores on the "Law and Order" test).

8. In adults, education more highly correlated than age to DIT scores. Adults seem to plateau in moral judgment development after leaving school. Following a group of senior high school subjects longitudinally, those who go on to college become increasingly divergent from their high school classmates who do not go on to college.

9. With directions to fake good, subjects' scores do not increase, but with directions to fake bad, subjects' scores decrease.

10. The DIT shows significant pre-post test gains in response to some educational experiences (e.g., an ethics course, A Deliberate Psychological Education Program) but not to other programs (art, logic, religion courses, 20-minute interventions).

11. The DIT has inconsistent or low correlations with many personality and attitude measures (e.g., Rotter's I-E Scale, Allport-Vernon-Lindsey Values Test, Tennessee Self Concept, Mach V, Hogan's S.E.A., Rokeach's Dogmatism, Political Efficacy or Trust, etc.), but significant correlations with some scales of the CPI and Omnibus Personality Inventory.

12. The DIT has shown significant relationships with experimental measures of behavior (sharing, cheating, or conformity behavior) and naturalistic measures of behavior (delinquency, voting in the 1976 presidential election, clinical ratings of doctors in a residency program, school behavior).

13. In 20 out of 22 studies, there are no significant sex differences; S.E.S. is moderately related to the DIT; geographical region of country and religious affiliation have a significant relation to the DIT. Religion can have either a retarding effect or facilitating effect, depending on how dogmatic or humanistic its stance on ethical issues.

14. Scaling studies show that the internal structure of responses to the DIT supports the theoretical sequence of the stages.

15. While related to purely cognitive variables and to some attitude variables, DIT scores are distinct from them and cannot be reduced to IQ, general cognitive or verbal ability, or to political attitudes.

As mentioned before, these studies are discussed in Rest (1979), along with an extensive reference list of the articles and dissertations which describe the studies in far more detail. (Also for those especially interested in higher education, see a more recent paper, "The Impact of Higher Education on Moral Judgment Development.") Contrary to a current widespread misconception, moral judgment research in the Kohlberg tradition has a very substantial data base with many replicated findings, with substantial numbers of subjects, and convergence on the crucial tenets of the cognitive developmental approach.

I'd like to make a few comments about using the DIT as a tool in evaluations of moral education and value education programs. (First, moral judgment is not the only component of moral development and therefore other assessments in addition to moral judgment should be included in evaluation of moral education programs.) I get the impression sometimes that some writers regard stages of moral judgment as an overall assessment of total personality organization—which is a gross overextension of the construct. Neverthless, this is not to deny the importance of moral judgment as a crucial aspect of moral development. Kohlberg's stages call attention to crucial inadequacies in moral reasoning at the lower stages and to crucial competence in envisioning cooperative structures at the higher stages. However we assess moral reasoning, moral justification, identifying relevant considerations, and integrating considerations, the distinctions which Kohlberg has embodied in his stage theory (which his test and the DIT key on) are critical features to attend to in apprasing moral development.

Second, it must be admitted that all current measures of moral judgment are broad-gauge, coarse-grained measures of moral thinking. The original research purpose of measures of moral judgment was to characterize the major epochs of life span development, not to provide a teacher with useful information about what to teach on next Tuesday afternoon. Longitudinal studies are usually conducted at 2 to 4 year intervals, not within the short intervals usually used by moral education programs. Given the coarse-grain measurement, change scores for any program of a year or less are bound to be undramatic. Indeed, if a 3-month program could move subjects from Stage 1 to Stage 6 it would be more of an invalidation of the theory and/or test than a testimony of program effectiveness. Perhaps the most consistent finding of studies using the DIT in educational evaluations is the recalcitrance of the DIT to change: no control groups in any of the studies (reviewed in Rest, 1979, Chapter 7) showed upward or downward change; only about half of the experimental groups showed significant pre-post change, and then only 5 to 12 points (about the average change in 2 to 4 years of normal development); none of the interventions produced students with scores like the moral philosopher-political science graduate students. It is not easy to get significant gains on the DIT with short term programs, especially if the program does not concentrate on a philosophical examination of reasoning about moral problems. On the other hand, we can be thankful for small favors, for no experimental group has changed DIT scores downward.

Third, if the DIT is used as an assessment tool, I strongly recommend that developmental theories about moral judgment not be part of the readings or discussions of the experimental group. Excluding such material prevents ambiguous interpretations of results (see Rest, 1979, p. 218-219).

Fourth, the distinct advantage of using the DIT in evaluation (aside from its ease of use) is the extensive research literature that can be related to score variance. The properties of DIT scores are pretty well known, its reliability well studied, and we know its major correlates. Ideally, students in an experimental educational program would be followed throughout their lives and contrasted to students not in the program. Such longitudinal studies are prohibitively costly, time-consuming, and difficult. The next best strategy is to demonstrate that the program produces changes on some well-researched variable with theoretical significance and known properties. Although we do not have research that shows that educational programs cause desirable life-long changes, we do have evidence that DIT scores are cumulative (i.e., upward changes don't wash out), that they are related to better conceptualization in moral reasoning, and are related to real-life moral behavior.

REFERENCES

Lockwood, A. "Relations of Political and Moral Thought." Unpublished doctoral dissertation, Harvard University, 1970.

Rest, J. R. Development in Judging Moral Issues. University of Minnesota Press, 1979. (2037 University Ave., S.E.; Minneapolis, Minn. 55414)

Rest, J. R. Revised Manual for the Defining Issues Test. Minnesota Moral Research Projects, 1979. (330 Burton Hall, 178 Pillsbury Drive, Minneapolis, Minn. 55455)

Rest, J. R. The Impact of Higher Education on Moral Judgment Development. Technical Report # 5, Minnesota Moral Research Projects, 1979. (330 Burton Hall, 178 Pillsbury Drive, Minneapolis, Minn. 55455)

Chapter 9

EXPLORATIONS INTO THE EVALUATION OF THE MORAL DEVELOPMENT OF PRE-ADOLESCENTS

James L. Carroll and Edward A. Nelsen

The influence of Lawrence Kohlberg's moral development theory and his painstaking refinement of criteria for the evaluation of moral growth has influenced not only the goals of many current moral education programs but has also manifested itself in the evaluation criteria of many programs. For many programs the success of the intervention has been judged on the basis of advancement in moral reasoning, despite the fact that such programs can and do have a variety of objectives and activities.

Ideally, evaluation will include measurement of each important goal and activity. Thus, if increased teacher skills in encouraging active listening, conflict resolution or cognitive dissidence are program goals, growth in such skills should be evaluated. If the range of objectives for students includes not only aspects of moral reasoning, but other educationally desirable variables such as comprehension of subject matter or development of basic interpersonal skills, these behaviors need to be evaluated.

The measures should be of such breadth and age appropriateness that they are sensitive to the effects of specific interventions. Short-term interventions may involve such limited experiences that it is unrealistic to expect substantial differences in terms of a broad measure of moral judgment development. Certainly, most developmental measures were not designed to assess short-term effects.

Furthermore, a single appraoch or assessment technique is unlikely to be equally appropriate and sensitive at all ages and levels of development. As Damon (1977) has indicated, " . . . if we are to study social knowledge across a span of development, we may be forced: (a) to observe different kinds of behavior in primitive and advanced persons and (b) to use different techniques to investigate these behaviors. It may be impossible, therefore, to 'standardize' an investigatory technique. One kind of question may best evoke a young child's knowledge about a certain social relation, whereas it may take an entirely different kind of question to tap an adult's knowledge of the same relation" (p. 45). Therefore, as robust as a structural sequence may be, attempts to generalize measures, interventions, and results across broad, developmentally active age spans seems inappropriate. Indeed, distinctions between ages are generally the core issue of developmental study, although they have sometimes been treated as a minor hazard (Arbuthnot, 1975).

Finally, evaluators should remain skeptical regarding the assumption that Kohlberg's conceptualization of sequential stages represents an exclusive basis for constructing interventions and measures. As Mischel (1979) has pointed out, there may be a validity in and appropriate uses for a variety of levels of categorization of person variables. In time, data may be developed that indicate that moral judgment stages are appropriate categories for long-term developmental analysis, but not particularly valuable for assessing and thinking about specific moral education program effects. Nevertheless, at present a structural view of moral development appears to have considerable empirical support (Rest, Panowitch, Balkcum and Davison), and data on alternative views are far from inclusive.

The test of a developmental measure is not, of course, only its internal consistency or relationship to other reasoning measures. Measures of reasoning must be related to other indices of moral development. Recent research on the relationship between attitude scales and behavior point to inadequate behavior sampling rather than inconsistency of attitudes or attitude measures as the basis for oft-cited moderate to small relationships between attitudes and behaviors (Weigel and Newman, 1976). Rest (1979) further discusses complexities in analyzing relationships of moral judgment development to other moral development processes and behavior. Additionally, in their social-learning analysis of punishment, Walters and Grusec (1977), argue, " . . . studies of moral behavior and moral judgment remained largely divorced from each other, being considered by many to be two unrelated aspects of development. However, it is apparent that the separation between them is not as complete as some may have thought."

ASSESSMENT OF MORAL JUDGMENT DEVELOPMENT FOR RESEARCH AND EVALUATION

For some age and ability groups several measures of moral judgment are available and have been shown to be sensitive and efficient enough to be used for program evaluation (Rest, 1979). For the intermediate and junior high school grades, however, moral judgment interviews, exemplified by Kohlberg's dilemmas and scoring system(s), provide the only well-documented procedure.

Studies using Kohlberg's Moral Judgment Interview or measures of moral comprehension indicate that students in the intermediate and early junior high school grades tend to use preconventional or conventional reasoning, especially Stages 2 and 3 (Holstein, 1976; Rothman, 1976). Dominance of Stage 4 reasoning and initial signs of principled reasoning appear somewhat later (Turiel, 1974). Measure of comprehension of and preference for stage prototypic reasons indicate parallel but somewhat higher levels of responding than spontaneous response measures for both pre-adolescents and adolescents (Rest, 1969, 1973). There are, of course, other measures based on the structural approach and utilizing similar interview measures and scoring systems (Adelson and O'Neil, 1966; Breznitz and Kugelmass, 1967; Eisenberg-Berg, 1976; Rest, Turiel and Kohlberg, 1969; Selman and Byrne; Turiel, 1978).

Such measures are time consuming and costly and cannot, at any price, be used appropriately to answer all the interesting and challenging questions that can be raised about moral judgment or moral development. What changes are occurring during the preadolescent years? How can one focus assessment on the essential changes? And, how can developmental progress be reasonably reliably and efficiently assessed in populations where there is great variability in reading achievement and cognitive development?

It is doubtful that new measures for preadolescents will be simply downward translations of measures available for older adolescents and adults. The task demands of present paper and pencil measures of moral judgment development preclude their use with younger children and less skilled readers. The task is not, however, to revise the existing measures to lower readability levels. New approaches are needed that use what we do know about preadolescent moral judgment and other aspects of cognitive development as bases for thorough assessment of developmentally relevant concepts.

AN ADDITIONAL APPROACH TO ASSESSING MORAL JUDGMENT DEVELOPMENT IN PREADOLESCENTS

At this point, I would like to present to you a convenient, inexpensive, valid instrument. However, I must instead settle for presenting a rationale and some data suggesting a possible line of attack on the problem of assessing moral judgment development in preadolescents. The basis for this approach is found in Piaget (1932) and has been repeatedly pointed out in cognitive developmental literature (Flavell, 1963, p. 201; Rest, 1969, p. 77). That is, one of the surest signs of developmental advance, whether cognitive or social-cognitive, is the clear rejection of lower stage, immature reasoning.

Thus, Piaget's subject, Fleu, (age 12) considers imminent justice an unacceptable, almost silly notion, " . . . the bridge was not supposed to know whether the boy had stolen apples." (Piaget, p. 257). The new conserver suddenly finds non-conserver reasoning rather amusing. Additionally, Laza-rowitz, Stephan and Friedman (1976) suggested that subjects at higher levels of reasoning respond negatively to reasoning below their own. Turiel (1974) also notes, "The hypothesis that emerges from the findings is that movement from one stage to the next is a process of rejection and construction: Through an awareness of its contradictions and inadequacies, the logic of the existing stage is rejected, and a new stage is then created" (p. 28).

Two steps have been taken toward better understanding of rejection of lower stage, prior reasoning as an interesting phenomenon in its own right and as a possible index of moral judgment development. In one study, (Carroll and Rest), students in Grades 7, 9 and 11 were asked to rate stage proto-typic moral advice statements on a four-point Likert type scale on a rejection to acceptance dimension. Four dilemmas were used, with ten items for each dilemma. Thus, eight items represented each of the first five stages. Rejection ratings assigned by students to statements representing stages one through four clearly discriminated age groups. In fact, considered separately, even the eight-item scales representing each of the lower stages yielded significant differences.

A number of findings from the Carroll and Rest study tended to support the possibility that rejection of prior stages of reasoning is a promising basis for understanding and assess-ing moral judgment. The internal consistency reliability of the scales representing each stage showed responses to items representing the first two stages to be more consistent (Stage 1, $r = .74$; Stage 2, $r = .72$) than responses to the highest stages (Stage 4, $r = .49$; Stage 5, $r = .56$). As was predicted for the age range studied, responses to items representing Stages 2, 3 and 4 yielded the greatest age effects (Stage 2, $> = 18.16$; Stage 3, $> = 21.75$; all P values $< .001$). The hypothesized pat-tern of greater association between adjacent stages and smaller relationships between the higher stages was also con-firmed.

The Carroll and Rest study, however, left a number of unanswered questions. Performance variations for different stories and alternative decisions were substantial and should have been controlled or treated as independent variables. While content may, for some researchers, be of greater interest than structure, the Carroll and Rest study can only indicate that structure and content each had significant effects on rejection rating responses for that sample. On the basis of research concerning same- and higher-stage reasons, Keasey (1973) said, "Clearly opinion/agreement rather than stage of supportive reasoning is the primary basis on which preadolescents evaluate moral arguments. It is possible that older subjects with more advanced cognitive and verbal abilities might rely more on reasoning when evaluating moral advice." However, his generalization does not appear to apply to preadolescents' evaluation of lower stage reasons.

Having obtained an initial indication that rejection data might prove interesting and useful, a second concern arose, i.e., What is the nature of children's rejections of prior, lower stage, reasoning? Accordingly, I have recently been collecting data to develop a taxonomy of reasons for rejection of prior, lower stage, reasoning.

Students in Grades 4, 6 and 8 are presented with several moral dilemmas. The dilemmas focus on different issues. After being asked to recall the story, the child is asked to describe what the central character ought to do. From that point on, the student is asked to make a series of paired comparison choices between advice statements (Sullivan). All alternatives support the action choice s/he made. The comparisons focus on the lower stages, e.g., 1 vs. 2, 1 vs. 3, 1 vs. 4, 2 vs. 3, 2 vs. 4, 3 vs. 4. Having chosen the advice statement which "gives the best reasons" the child is then asked: (a) to explain what it was about the other statement, the statement they did not choose, that made them decide to reject it, and (b) to attempt to restate the rejected statement to make it as good or better than the chosen statement. Additional problem questions were also piloted, e.g., "Describe a person who would give the reasons in advice statement A. What about the statement makes you think that?"

Preliminary data indicate that a taxonomy will include

nonmoral as well as moral reasons for rejection and may reflect content or issue differences even when action choice is controlled. Rather than present tentative or speculative findings, let me describe the working hypotheses: (a) the greater the span between the contrasting stages, the lower the likelihood that nonmoral reasons will be given for rejection decisions, (b) older children will reject lower stage reasons with greater consistency and will provide more specific reasons for their rejection decisions, (c) children will be able to amend or restate advice statements so as to raise the level at which they would be scored, and (d) older students will be more successful in revising low stage items to the level of the higher stage comparison.

CONCLUSION

There is much yet to be learned about moral development. Some of what we need to know involves children's responses to and thinking about moral problems and moral reasoning. Some of it involves a more precise fit between children's general cognitive and emotional development and the instruments best able to tap their characteristic modes of thinking. By limiting assessment to changes tapped by a spontaneous production measure and by using scoring systems that have tended to define away lower stage responses, highly significant programmatic effects may have been missed. As Keasey (1977) has noted in regard to Piaget's intent/consequence dilemmas, "for new questions, new paradigms are needed" (p. 232), and, "In response to the question of which index is best, one would have to counter with 'For what?'" (p. 252). With regard to preadolescent moral judgment development, the question is not yet "Which index is best?" Rather, the issue is: What other indices make sense theoretically, and when will we get on with the task of instrument development and evaluation?

Moral judgment development undoubtedly involves production of reasons at new, higher stages. It has long been held that progress also involves consolidation at the modal stage or highest stage of significant use. It seems possible that progress should also be reflected in increased discrimination and meaningful rejection of prior, lower stage, reasoning.

REFERENCE NOTES

1. Rest, J. R., Panowitsch, H., Balkcum, E., and Davison, M. "The Relation of Moral Judgment to Cognitive Development: Looking for Dr. Strangelove." Unpublished manuscript, University of Minnesota, 1979.

2. Selman, R. L., and Byrne, D. "Manual for Scoring Role-Taking in Social and Moral Judgment Interviews." Unpublished manuscript, Harvard University, 1973.

3. Carroll, J. L., and Rest, J. R. "Development in Moral Judgment as Indicated by Rejection of Lower Stage Statements." Manuscript submitted for publication, 1979.

4. Sullivan, A. P. "Measurement of Moral Judgment: Using Stimulus Pairs to Estimate Inter-Judge Distances." Paper presented to the American Educational Research Association, Toronto, 1978.

REFERENCES

Adelson, J., and O'Neil, R. P. "The Growth of Political Ideas in Adolescence: The Sense of Community. *Journal of Personality and Social Psychology*, 1966, 4, 295-306.

Arbuthnot, J. "Modification of Moral Judgment Through Role Playing." *Developmental Psychology*, 1975, 11, 319-324.

Breznitz, S., and Kugelmass, S. "Intentionality in Moral Judgment: Developmental Stages." *Child Development*, 1967, 38, 469-479.

Damon, W. **The Social World of the Child**. San Francisco: Jossey-Bass, 1977.

Eisenberg-Berg, N. "The Relation of Political Attitudes to Constraint-Oriented and Prosocial Moral Reasoning." *Developmental Psychology*, 1976, 12, 552-553.

Flavell, J. H. **The Developmental Psychology of Jean Piaget**. Princeton, New York: Van Nostrand-Reinhold, 1963.

Holstein, C. B. "Irreversible, Stepwise Sequence in the Development of Moral Judgment: A Longitudinal Study of Males and Females." *Child Development*, 1976, 47, 51-61.

Keasey, C. B. "Experimentally Induced Changes in Moral Opinions and Reasoning." *Journal of Personality and Social Psychology*, 1973, 26, 30-38.

Keasey, C. B. "Children's Developing Awareness and Usage of Intentionality and Motives." In C. B. Keasey (Ed.), **Nebraska Symposium on Motivation**, Vol. 25. Lincoln: University of Nebraska Press, 1977.

Lazarowitz, R., Stephan, W. G., and Friedman, S. T. "Effects of Moral Justifications and Moral Reasoning on Altruism." *Developmental Psychology*, 1976, 12, 353-354.

Mischel, W. "On the Interface of Cognition and Personality: Beyond the Person-Situation Debate." *American Psychologist*, 1979, 34, 740-754.

Munson, H. "Moral Thinking: Can it be Taught?" *Psychology Today*, 1979, Vol. 12, 48-92.

Nelsen, E. "Evaluation Planning for Humanities and Law Related Education Programs for Elementary School Children." In L. C. Falkenstein and C. C. Anderson (Eds.), **Law and Humanities in the Elementary School**, American Bar Association Special Committee on Youth Education for Citizenship (in press).

Piaget, J. **The Moral Judgment of the Child** (M. Gabain, trans.). New York: The Free Press, 1965. (Originally published, 1932.)

Rest, J. "Patterns of Preference and Comprehension in Moral Judgment." *Journal of Personality*, 1973, 41, 86-109.

Rest, J. **Development in Judging Moral Issues**. Minneapolis: University of Minnesota Press, 1979.

Rest, J., Turiel, E., and Kohlberg, L. "Relations between Level of Moral Judgment and Preference and Comprehension of the Moral Judgment of Others." *Journal of Personality*, 1969, 37, 225-252.

Rothman, G. R. "The Influence of Moral Reasoning on Behavioral Choices." *Child Development*, 1976, 47, 397-406.

Turiel, E. "Conflict and Transition in Adolescent Moral Development." *Child Development*, 1974, 45, 14-29.

Turiel, E. "The Development of Concepts of Social Structure: Social Convention." In J. Glick and K. A. Clarke-Stewart (Eds.), **The Development of Social Understanding.** New York: Gardner Press, 1978.

Walker, L. J., and Richards, B. S. "Stimulating Transitions in Moral Reasoning as a Function of Stage of Cognitive Development." *Developmental Psychology*, 1979, **15,** 95-103.

Walters, G. C., and Grusec, J. E. **Punishment.** San Francisco: W. H. Freeman, 1977.

Weigel, R. H., and Newman, L. S. "Increasing Attitude-Behavior Correspondence by Broadening the Scope of the Behavioral Measure." *Journal of Personality and Social Psychology*, 1976, **33,** 793-802.

Chapter 10

ISSUES AT THE INTERFACE OF SCIENCE, TECHNOLOGY AND SOCIETY

Louis A. Iozzi and June Paradise-Maul

MORAL DILEMMAS AND SCIENTIFIC RESPONSIBILITY

That we live in a technological society during a technological era cannot be debated. However, whether or not we
actually want to live in this type of technological society or
during this technological era is a separate issue, one which
many of us consider a moral issue. Some citizens are quick
to identify science and technology as the culprits responsible
for pollution, the population explosion, the horrors related
to chemical and germ warfare, proliferation of nuclear power,
as well as the forecasted atrocities of genetic engineering and
a variety of recent biological discoveries. However, responsibility implies "having a capacity for moral decisions."
Neither science nor technology, and thus neither the scientist
or technologist alone (per se), has this capacity. Rather, it is
the decision-makers and policy-makers involved in the application of science and technology to social issues, and the
citizens who delegate or permit them to make social policy,
who are actually *morally responsible*.

The all-pervasive influence of science and technology in
our society places a demand of moral responsibility not
only on scientists as decision-makers and/or policy-makers
but also on the politicians and citizens who have placed them
in their roles. Moral dilemmas involving research in science,
the application of technology, as well as the responsibility of

131

politicians, scientists and citizens exist today and will continue to exist in the future. Incorporation of these "real world" moral dilemmas into the science curriculum in our schools is the best method to prepare the students of today to effectively deal with the social and moral responsibilities as politicians or as scientists or as citizens of the future.

In an attempt to meet this need, Louis Iozzi and the members of the Institute for Science, Technology and Social Science Education have developed a fourteen module curriculum project, *Preparing for Tomorrow's World*, which addresses ethical issues at the interface of science, technology and society. In order to assess the effect of these curriculum materials on the development of social/moral reasoning Louis Iozzi used an instrument similar to James Rest's *Defining Issues Test* (DIT) entitled *The Environmental Issues Test* (EIT), which is described in the following pages. Although this instrument has proven satisfactory for evaluation/research in Grades ten through twelve, its complex design has made it unsatisfactory for use with students in Grades 7 through 9. At the end of the article, a junior version of this instrument, currently being constructed, is described.

EVALUATING GROWTH IN THE CAPACITY
TO REASON ABOUT SCIENTIFIC ISSUES

Moral reasoning levels have been typically assessed by Kohlberg and his colleagues using the moral judgment interview (Kohlberg, 1963). However, this is a laborious and time-consuming task since it is a clinical interview administered on a one-to-one basis, requiring highly trained interviewers with an in-depth knowledge of the scoring protocol. An alternative is James Rest's *Defining Issues Test* (an objective paper and pencil test) (Rest, 1973), based on Kohlberg's dilemma stories. This instrument taps an individual's preference for a particular mode of reasoning on moral issues. However, the specificity of the test raises certain methodological concerns. For example, in explaining horizontal decalage in the development of logical reasoning, Piaget observes that people tend to reason at higher levels in those areas in which they have great knowledge or experience (Piaget, 1972). This suggests that the context and issues about which one reasons can influence the maturity level of the response.

That this decalage is also evident in the moral-ethical reasoning sphere was elucidated by Iozzi in studies conducted in 1975 and 1976 (Iozzi, 1976). In his studies the responses to the Rest *Defining Issues Test* (DIT) were compared to the Iozzi instrument, *The Environmental Issues Test* (EIT). The EIT differed from the Rest DIT only in that the dilemma story is changed. The issue statement, which respondents evaluate, remained essentially identical. The study revealed that people reason at different moral levels on moral issues set in a different context. Environmental Science majors at a large eastern university, in contrast to students at the same school majoring in the Humanities, received significantly higher scores on the EIT than on the DIT. That is, Environmental Science majors selected more higher stage issue statements when they responded to the dilemma based on an environmental issue and selected fewer higher stage statements on dilemma stories based on general social issues. The study attributed this difference to the fact that Environmental Science majors more familiar with Environmental issues were significantly more knowledgeable, possessed greater interest in, concern for, and commitment to, environmental causes than were the Humanities majors.

The Environmental Issues Test

The EIT is comprised of five dilemma stories each of which highlights an environmental issue and the moral conflicts inherent in that issues. Following each dilemma story is a series of twelve issue statements, each keyed to a specific moral reasoning stage as defined by Kohlberg. Respondents are asked to assign a priority rating (from *greatest* to *no importance*, a four-category scale) to each statement in terms of its relative degree of importance in making a particular decision. Based on this rating they then select the four most important, ranked in their order of priority. Each dilemma is scored in terms of the moral reasoning level of the four most important statements selected with relative weighting given to each rank. An individual's reasoning level is obtained by adding the scores on all the dilemma stories tested.

Validation of the EIT

Is the EIT a valid instrument to assess moral judgment levels? Because of its obvious parallel construction to Rest's *Defining Issues Test*, the EIT possesses "face validity." However, it is also important to determine the construct validity of the instrument. In other words, does the instrument provide a measurement of the psychological construct, moral judgment? (Cronbach and Meehl, 1955; Rest, 1976). Using the same procedures established by Rest, the validity of the EIT was determined by the following criteria (Iozzi, 1976):

1. Test-retest stability

2. Age trends

3. Correlation with attitudes on current environmental issues (Maloney, 1971; Maloney and Ward, 1973)

4. Correlation with comprehension of moral concepts

5. Correlation with existing moral judgment measures (Rest, 1973)

Applicability of the EIT

Since tests of construct validity supported the contention that the EIT measures levels of moral/ethical judgment for moral issues set in an environmental context, the EIT has been used extensively to assess the effectiveness of the *Preparing for Tomorrow's World Program*, a 14-module curriculum project for Grades 7 through 12. The advantages of this test lie in the fact that it provides baseline information quickly and easily. Moreover, its method of scoring permits investigators to detect small increments of change. This is especially important for short-term interventions where one cannot expect a full-stage shift from one stage to the next, since stage changes occur gradually over periods of years. Change, as detected with EIT, is based on what is termed the "P" Score. The "P" Score is interpreted as the relative importance, expressed as percentage, an individual gives to morally principled considerations in making moral judgments. This scoring procedure, in contrast to stage scoring, allows for detection of small changes within a stage.

In addition, baseline data on the range and sequence of concepts comprehensible to secondary school students facilitates the design of activities and teaching strategies that best match younger students' capabilities and environmental perspectives. At the junior high school level, concepts may need to be presented in a more interactive and concrete manner than at the senior high school level, where the more mature students comprehend concepts presented through written materials with greater ease.

An EIT Designed for the Lower Grades—The Junior EIT

James Rest has encountered a number of difficulties using the DIT with students below the ninth grade, and we have experienced similar problems with the EIT. First, the test format requiring students to assign priorities to the twelve issue statements and rank order the four most important is, for the most part, an unfamiliar task. Students seem to find great difficulty translating the priority rating into useful information to help them select and rank order the four most important statements.

Second, the large number of issue statements appear to tax the attention span of younger students, and as a result they have difficulty making their selections. Fortunately, the scoring procedure permits identification of those students who make random selections. Applying this screening process, 20% to 30% of the tests are typically discarded. In addition, some students complete the prioritizing section but ignore the final ranking, the part which is scored.

Third, a higher proportion of the issue statements are keyed for Stages 4, 5 and 6 and do not measure with great sensitivity the reasoning level of younger students. Also, these statements, to some degree, are written in language too difficult for younger students to understand. Hence, they fail to correnctly interepret the meaning of the statements, even though it is possible that they have some understanding or preference for those concepts.

A more appropriate test for the younger age group should: 1) contain a greater number of statements keyed to a less sophisticated level of reasoning; 2) be written in simpler language; 3) have a less complex testing procedure to follow; and 4) have a more simplified and manageable method of scoring (i.e., a test which can be machined scored rather than hand scored, which is the case with the EIT and DIT). The Junior version of the EIT which is in development will fulfill all of the above conditions.

The basic structure of the Junior EIT will be a series of dilemma stories, each followed by a set of questions. Answers to the questions will be selected from among four possible choices. The questions will be based on the probe questions used in the clinical interview. Respondents will select from among the possible choices the one they believe best resolves the question. Each of these answers is derived from the set of typical responses previously identified and staged typed. The score obtained will reflect the dominant moral reasoning stage an individual employs to identify what s/he holds to be the most important considerations in making judgments. By examining the component scores, we can obtain a more definitive picture of a person's reasoning level as well as detect the subtle changes that occur between levels following intervention studies.

CONCLUSIONS

We are not aware of any other instruments presently available which are designed to assess moral/ethical reasoning within an environmental context. This gap can be met with

with EIT and the Junior EIT, which address science and
technology issues within an environmental context. These
two instruments, we believe, can serve as important research
and evaluation tools. Knowledge acquisition is for the most
part easily measured. However, if the moral/ethical dimension is an equally important factor in the education of a
responsible and contributing citizenry, we need to better
understand the developmental process of this thought component, and provide those experiences that will facilitate
continuous upward growth.

REFERENCES

Iozzi, Louis A. "The Environmental Issues Test (EIT): A New Assessment Instrument for Environmental Education." **Current Issues in
Environmental Education** - IV. Craig B. Davis and Arthus Sacks
(Eds.). Columbus, Ohio: ERIC Clearinghouse for Science, Mathematics, and Environmental Education, 1978, pp. 200-206.

Iozzi, Louis A. "Moral Judgment, Verbal Ability, Logical Reasoning
Ability, and Environmental Issues." Unpublished doctoral dissertation, Rutgers, The State University of New Jersey, 1976.

Kohlberg, Lawrence, "Moral Stages and Moralization: The Cognitive-
Developmental Approach." **Moral Development and Behavior:
Theory, Research, and Social Issues.** Thomas Lickona (Ed.) New
York: Holt, Rinehart, and Winston, 1976, pp. 31-53.

Kohlberg, Lawrence, "Moral Development and Identification." In H.
Stevenson (Ed.). **Child Psychology: The Sixty-second Yearbook of
the National Society for the Study of Education.** Chicago, Illinois:
The University of Chicago Press, 1963.

Kohlberg, Lawrence, et. al. **Moral Judgment Interview Scoring Manual.**
Cambridge, Mass: Center for Moral Education, Harvard University,
1978.

Piaget, Jean, "Intellectual Evolution from Adolescence to Adulthood."
Human Development 15, pp. 1-12, 1972.

Rest, James R., "New Approaches in the Assessment of Moral Judgment." **Moral Development and Behavior: Theory, Research, and
Social Issues.** Thomas Lickona (Ed.). New York: Holt, Rinehart,
and Winston, 1976, pp. 198-218.

Rest, James R., "The Validity of Tests of Moral Judgment," **Values Education: Theory, Practice, Problems, Prospectives.** J. Meyer, B. Burnham, and J. Cholvats (Eds.). Waterloo, Canada: Walford Laurier University Press, 1975, pp. 103-116.

Rest, James R., Douglas Casper, Richard Coder, and Joanna Coder, "Devising and Evaluating an Objective Test of Moral Judgment for Adolescents and Adults." Unpublished mimeographed paper, University of Minnesota, 1973.

Chapter 11

THE ETHICAL REASONING INVENTORY

James R. Bode and Roger A. Page

WHY A NEW MEASURE?

Our early research in measuring moral reasoning at first utilized the Kohlberg (1958) Moral Judgment Interview (MJI) exclusively. To circumvent some of the problems associated with the interview (e.g., time-consuming administration, transcribing of protocols for scoring, etc.) we tried the Moral Judgment Scale (MJS) of Maitland and Goldman (1974). We quickly found, however, that the MJS simply did not discriminate subjects, not even those varying widely in grade and age level. As a result, we became interested in developing a paper-and-pencil measure of moral reasoning that would incorporate the following features:

1) quick and easy group administration;

2) a recognition task for objective scoring (manually or by machine);

3) an index equivalent to the moral maturity score of the MJI.

These concerns led us to develop a new instrument which we named the Ethical Reasoning Inventory (ERI).

NATURE OF THE INSTRUMENT

In 1976 we began to develop the ERI and in 1978 we finished our preliminary testing (Page and Bode, in press). This instrument is an objective group-administered measure employing six Kohlberg dilemmas from the MJI (Dilemmas I, II, III, IV, VII, VIII) and prototypic statements representing Stages 1 through 5 drawn from a set of standard scoring manuals (Kohlberg, 1973). The prototypic statements were condensations of actual responses and their summary descriptions found in the manuals. For example, Question 5 in the MJI "Heinz" dilemma (described elsewhere, e.g., Kohlberg, 1969, p. 379) is: "Suppose he was stealing it (the drug) for a pet he loved dearly. Would it be right to steal for the pet? Why?" Descriptions and some sample Stage 3 responses found on pages 18 and 19 (Form A) are as follows:

C.10   It might be right to steal to save its life because the attachment could be great enough (stresses how great an attachment can be to a pet).

Examples: "People don't put a price on love whether or not it is a human life or a pet."

"Yes, people can get so attached to an animal that they treat them like members of the family instead of animals. Animals are the greatest comfort to loneliness."

C.11   An animal is a living being, too, and because it is suffering, should be helped.

Examples: "If there was no other way, maybe yes. It is a living creature and they should be spared."

"Yes, a pet is a life and they want to live, too, and if you loved the pet, you're going to do all in your power to save him."

The condensed Stage 3 statement to the same question in the ERI is:

"Because people can get so attached to an animal that it's almost like a member of the family to them. People don't put a price on love whether it's a human life or a pet; an animal is a living being, too, and because it's suffering it should be helped."

A successful effort was made to construct Stage 3, 4, and 5 tatements of approximately the same average length, but Stage 1 and 2 statements were shorter on the average.

A total of 26 questions are asked over the six dilemmas, with 14 of these employing a branching technique. For example, to the question, "Suppose he was stealing it for a pet he loved dearly. Would it be right to steal it for the pet?", the subject can check either "yes" or "no." The subject is instructed to turn to page 8 if "yes" is checked and to page 9 if "no" is checked. Here statements representing the different stages, as well as "nonsense" statements (to check for careless or random answering) and "abstract" statements (to check for endorsement of complex-sounding statements) are found. The remaining 12 questions do not branch and are simply followed by a set of statements representing the stages with some nonsense and abstract responses mixed in. The percentage of possible responses representing Stages 1 through 5 for the entire ERI (a total of 188 state statements) is 18.1%, 21.3%, 21.3%, 20.7%, and 18.6% respectively. A subject's ERI score is simply the average of his/her stage selections.

The ERI thus allows a subject to place himself/herself among possible prototypic statements. The placement is, however, a forced choice and there may be cases in which the subject finds no choice which reflects exactly what s/he would say. In such a case the subject decides which statement is closest to what s/he wishes to say. We suppose that the untutored subject is able, when presented with alternate choices, none of which matches the words s/he would use, to decide which alternative is closest to his/her thinking by in effect trying them out.

Occasionally this forced choice undoubtedly results in instances where the subject reads something into a statement which was not intended; in each such case this would result in one inappropriate stage level mark. However, the high level of internal consistency of the ERI (to be discussed) convinces us that these occasions are rare enough to insure that the ERI constitutes a reliable measure of Kohlberg-type stage levels. Yet the clustering of responses at more than one stage leads us to believe that a phenomenon similar to that which Piaget calls "decalage" is occurring here. Subject's moral reasoning appears to be characterizable as having reached a certain level of understanding represented by the central tendency of the measure; however, s/he may not have learned to apply this understanding successfully in some areas even though s/he has done so in other areas. Thus, we believe that all the subject's stage markings should be taken into account to assess not only the subject's bare understanding of a stage but also how successfully and thoroughly s/he has applied that understanding to varying ethical situations.

The ERI should be viewed as one of a range of instruments available to assess moral reasoning. It has the advantage of ease of administration and machine scorability; to gain these advantages it perforce sacrifices certain depth and detail which are available in other instruments that are more difficult to administer and interpret. The experimenter must be guided in choosing the appropriate instrument by the available time, budget, and above all the purpose for which the test is being given.

VALIDATION RESEARCH

Our validation research, still in its initial stage, has focused on the following types of data:

1) Internal consistency;

2) Temporal stability;

3) Age trends;

4) Correlations with other measures of moral reasoning;

5) Correlations with other theoretically related measures;

6) Susceptibility to faking;

7) Sensitivity of the ERI to induced changes in moral reasoning.

Internal Consistency

In our original validation study with college subjects (Page & Bode, in press), we found the item-total correlations (treating each dilemma average as an item) ranged from .12 to .52 with a median of .49; the Cronbach Alpha for the six dilemmas was .69 and was improved to .74 by deleting the least related dilemma (No. 4 on euthanasia). Taking each of the 26 responses as separate measures resulted in item-total correlations ranging from .08 to .60 with a median of .28; the Cronbach Alpha was .75 and was imporoved slightly to .77 by deletion of the least related item (Item 16 in the fourth dilemma).

Temporal Stability

Thus far, we have three sets of data pertaining to test-retest reliability. The first set consists of scores on 51 subjects from one of the samples of college students in the original validation study mentioned above. A Pearson product-moment correlation of .69 was obtained for scores over a test-retest interval of 10 days. A second set of data consists of scores on 54 college subjects who served as controls in a study of the susceptibility to faking of the ERI (Page & Bode, 1979). With a seven-day test-retest interval, a Pearson correlation of .80 was obtained. The third set of data is from a recently completed study (Page & Bode, in preparation) which employed 40 college students as controls. Scores over a ten-week test-retest interval produced a Pearson correlation of .69. Group means did not differ significantly over any of the intervals.

Age Trends

In our original validation sample of 92 students, we found a Pearson correlation between age and ERI of .29, comparing favorably with the MJI (r = .34) for the same sample. Correlations for six other groups that we have examined are .40, .40, .38, .26, and .08.

Table 1
Age and ERI Means in Groups Studied

Group	N	Mean ERI	Mean Age
High School	78	3.40	15.94
College Freshman	70	3.57	18.83
College Students	58	3.57	19.40
College Students	54	3.60	20.30
College Students	69	3.61	20.10
College Students	92	3.63	22.28
College Students	51	3.68	21.35
College Students	40	3.72	24.08
College Students	32	3.73	22.78
College Students	62	3.73	23.36

Table 1 presents the mean ERI score and mean age of several groups we have thus far studied. All but one group are college students. The non-college group (78 9th through 12th grade males) has scored significantly lower on the ERI than any of our college groups, including entering freshmen. Inspection of Table 1 shows the general trend of higher age with higher ERI score; the data produce a rank difference correlation of .93.

Correlations with Other Measures of Moral Reasoning

Table 2 contains the Pearson correlations for the MJI, ERI, DIT, and MJS that we obtained in the original validation study. Although all measures correlated significantly, the ERI and DIT were more strongly related to the MJI than was the MJS. The ERI had a slightly higher correlation with the MJI than the DIT did, but the highest correlation was between the ERI and DIT. This may be due in part to the fact that both measures are recognition tasks rather than spontaneous production tasks. The somewhat higher MJI/ERI correlation may be due in part to the fact that both measures employ the same dilemmas while the DIT contains only three (slightly modified) MJI dilemmas.

Table 2

Pearson Correlations Between Measures

Measure	1	2	3
1. MJI	-----		
2. ERI	.54**	-----	
3. DIT	.50**	.57**	-----
4. MJS	.26*	.43**	.26*

*p<.02   **p<.001

Note: p score is index used for DIT.
(Taken from Educational and Psychological Measurement, in press.)

An additional set of data stems from the previously mentioned high school sample (Bode & Page, in press) in which we found a Pearson correlation of .39 between MJI and ERI. Combining the two sets of data (high school and original validation sample) produced an overall correlation of .56 between the two measures.

Correlations with Other Theoretically Related Measures

Thus far, we have two sets of data relevant in this area drawn from previously cited studies (Page and Bode, in press; Bode & Page, in press). The first set produced a Pearson correlation of -.32 between the ERI and California F Scale (Adorno, Frenkel-Brunswik, Levinson, & Sanford, 1950), while the second set produced a correlation of -.21 between the ERI and short-form Dogmatism Scale (Troldahl & Powell, 1965). Considering the nature of these two scales, the relationships are in the expected direction.

Susceptibility to Faking

Since the ERI is a recognition task, the possibility of faking (selecting either higher or lower stage reasoning) arises. To test this possibility, we had groups attempt to "fake good" or "fake bad" (i.e., they were told to imagine that in order to obtain a job, they had to identify the best or the worst ethical reasoning on a test), and we compared these attempts to their scores under standard instructions and to a test-retest control group. Results (Page & Bode, 1979) were similar to those found by McGeorge (1975) for the DIT: while the "fake good" group was unable to raise their scores, the "fake bad" group was able to lower their scores significantly.

Sensitivity to Induced Changes in Moral Reasoning

In a study just completed (Page & Bode, in preparation), we tested the sensitivity of the ERI to any changes in moral reasoning that might be induced through college ethics classes (ten weeks in length).

The ethics course emphasized the logical analysis of normative ethical positions. Various historical positions (ethical egoism, utilitarianism, kantianism, etc.) were represented within a general schema which organized normative theories in terms of such characteristics as the types of rules they used and the kinds of things counted as morally relevant (consequences, motives, etc.). The students were taught to evaluate these theories in terms of their adequacy in explaining moral phenomena (that people disagree on some singular moral judgments, that they agree on many other singular moral judgments, that they offer certain kinds of facts in support of their ethical opinions, etc.). The emphasis in the course was on logical analysis and rational argument.

In particular, there was no discussion of Kohlberg's stage theories or of any dilemmas of the sort used in stage assessment. The intention was to make very certain that any changes which occurred in stage level were the result of genuine change and not the result of the student's learning to simulate higher stages. Since the students had taken the ERI at the beginning of the course, there were some questions raised about the dilemmas during the course. Whenever this happened, the question was simply turned away by saying that the question was not appropriate at this time and perhaps could be considered later.

An introductory psychology class (in which the topic of moral development was not touched upon) served as a control group. The difference between pre-test means for the ethics and control groups (3.7; 3.7) was not significant ($T_{70} = .20$, P = .84).

At the conclusion of the quarter, we found the difference between pre- and post-test ethics means (3.7; 3.9) was significant ($T_{31} = 3.99$, P < .001), while that for the control means (3.7; 3.7) was not ($T_{39} = .20$, P = .84). The ethics subjects showed a higher percentage of upward change (69% increased, 22% decreased, 9% were unchanged) than the control subjects (47.5% increased, 35% decreased, 17.5% were unchanged), with both ethics and control groups showing a high degree of correlation between pre- and post-test scores (.82, P < .001; .69, P < .001).

Thus, the study appears to establish both that the ERI is sufficiently sensitive to measure induced changes in moral reasoning and that a course in the analysis of historical ethical positions will induce development within the Kohlbergian framework.

CONCLUSIONS

The ERI provides a mass-administrable machine-scorable measure of the moral reasoning of subjects which have been tested in administrations ranging from 9th grade students through adults. It is designed to yield a measure which is comparable to Kohlberg's MMS score and to be used in situations where the use of the Kohlberg interview measure is impractical.

While the validation research is still in its preliminary stages, we are encouraged with the results we have in hand and have described. Other studies that we have under way include longitudinal use of the ERI, exploring its relationship to personality dimensions, extending its use beyond the high school and undergraduate level, and examining the way in which subjects rank the different stage statements on the ERI.

Other investigators are beginning to employ the ERI and their results will be helpful in confirming or disconfirming the general usefulness of the instrument.

REFERENCES

Adorno, T. W., Frenkel-Brunswik, E., Levinson, D. J. & Sanford, R. N. **The Authoritarian Personality**. Harper, New York, 1950.

Bode, J. & Page, R. "Further Validation of the Ethical Reasoning Inventory." *Psychological Reports,* in press.

Kohlberg, L. "The Development of Modes of Moral Thinking and Choice in the Years Ten to Sixteen." Unpublished doctoral dissertation, University of Chicago, 1958.

Kohlberg, L. "Stage and Sequence: the Cognitive-Developmental Approach to Socialization." In D. A. Goslin (Ed.), **Handbook of Socialization Theory and Research**. Rand McNally, Chicago, 1969, pp. 347-480.

Kohlberg, L. "Standard Scoring Manual for the Moral Judgment Interview." Unpublished manuscript, Harvard University, 1973.

Maitland, K. A. & Goldman, J. R. "Moral Judgment as a Function of Peer Group Interaction." *Journal of Personality and Social Psychology*, 1974, **30**, pp. 699-704.

McGeorge, C. "Susceptibility to Faking of the Defining Issues Test of Moral Development." *Developmental Psychology,* 1975, 11, p. 108.

Page, R. & Bode, J. "Degree of Susceptibility to Faking of the Ethical Reasoning Inventory." *Journal of Educational Research,* 1979, 72, pp. 355-356.

Page, R. & Bode, J. "Comparison of Measures of Moral Reasoning and Development of a New Objective Measure." *Educational and Psychological Measurement,* in press.

Page, R. & Bode, J. "Inducing Changes in Moral Reasoning." (In preparation.)

Troldahl, V. & Powell, F. A. "A Short-Form Dogmatism Scale for Use in Field Studies." *Social Forces,* 1965, 44, pp. 211-214.

Chapter 12

THE CASE STUDY METHOD
IN THE EVALUATION OF
DEVELOPMENTAL PROGRAMS

V. Lois Erickson

John Dewey, whose claim, " . . . true education is development," provides the underlying premise of this book, has also advised educational researchers that if a search is "not to lead us into the clouds (we must discover) what actually takes place when education really occurs."

The central thesis of this chapter is that if we are to ever find out what actually takes place through developmental interventions, we must consider all the ways in which we can get information from curriculum studies. In particular, we must try to seek more of the "whole truth" and recognize the importance of "coefficients of completeness" (Kounin, 1975).

In this paper I will:

Stress the importance of including case studies of individual students' growth in the evaluation of developmental interventions such that a methodology valuing completeness becomes an integrated part of the design.

Stress the necessity of using theoretical constructs to analyze themes in case studies such that the methodology itself employs appropriate intellectual heft;

Share with you representative excerpts from longitudinal case studies selected from my annual five year follow-up data on 21 young women who participated in an experimental developmental education course.

THE NEED FOR INTEGRATING CASE STUDY DATA INTO DEVELOPMENTAL EDUCATION EVALUATION

During the past five or six years I have taught or team taught five experimental courses in the public schools, advised and coadvised several other curriculum intervention thesis studies, and facilitated numerous training workshops for teachers and state department curriculum directors. The main point I want to share with you from my own field-based research experiences is that, again and again, I have been dismayed that the global statistical pre/post assessments of experimental projects capture very little of what "actually takes place when developmental education really occurs."

John Gibbs' (1979) article on ecological oriented inquiry, Robert Stake's (1978) article on the case study method, and Klaus Riegel's (1976) interpretations of the dialectics of the change process are all helpful sources for understanding the need for exploratory, in-depth hypotheses generating research at this pioneer phase of applied developmental psychology.

The state of the art in developmental education is such that we are still mapping out a largely uncharted process. While the structural stage conceptions of Piaget, Kohlberg, and Loevinger provide important milestones for theoretically visualizing some successful outcomes of developmental interventions, the labor we are about—clinically teaching for structural change—is yet barely understood. The complexity and mystery of the structural change process looms before us:

What principle is at the core of the "qualitative level of organization?"

What are the mechanisms of a "structural change?"

How does a teacher/experimenter "know" what is appropriate dissonance, disequilibrium, cognitive-mismatch?

What are the necessary time parameters in the transformations of stages? What are the minimal time requirements for individual persons that can't be modified by planned developmental curriculum?

What do we really know about the bridge between reasoning and behavior?

What about the presence of pathology in the midst of cognitive maturity?

Do affects, defenses also have an invariant order? How do they impact upon structural change?

How does motivation for change affect structural transformation?

If we are to intervene in a humane fashion, I believe we need to maintain a stance of humility and do our very best to balance the race for rigorous scientific explanation with careful attention to how this process of developmental intervention is experienced by the participants.

Klaus Riegel (1976) wrote, "Pay serious attention to the application of biographical inquiries by which the individual does not only continue to reconstruct his (sic) own past but by which he also can construct his future in changing forms and with never ceasing hope" (p. 698). The forms and order that our students construct as they participate in our experimental classes extend far beyond that recorded in the specific assessment instruments we have selected. We need to better capture their personal accounts of this change process.

DEVELOPMENTAL CASE STUDY METHOD:
THE USE OF THEORETICAL CONSTRUCTS
TO EXAMINE CENTRAL THEMES IN THE DATA

In this section I will identify some of the sorting variables helpful in the developmental analysis of selected themes in case study data. I will also try to capture examples from three case study reports as they relate to each theme. However, first, a quick sketch of the background of this case study research project and some general background data on the three participants will create a context for viewing their lives in progress.

The Case Study Research Project

Over the past several months I have begun individual case study analysis of selected young women who were participants in a developmental education class which I taught in 1973 which was designed to promote women's developmental growth. The 23 young women who took part in the experimental class were then high school sophomores in the inner-city school where this course was offered as an elective part of the humanities curriculum. The experimental course is reviewed in Erickson (1977a). Over the next five years, 21 of the 23 participants took part in an annual follow-up study in which I gathered their responses to several self-report questionnaires and also to a moral judgment test (Kohlberg written interviews) and an ego integration measure (Loevinger/Wessler Sentence Completion Test). A brief summary of some of the key theoretical relationships apparent between the ego and moral domains can be found in Erickson (1977b). The five year annual ego and moral data on this group of 21 young women is included in Appendices A and B. This data was all rescored in 1978 to update the scoring methods and to get rater consistency across the data pool.[1]

Some Characteristics of the Case Study Participants
and the Role of The Researcher

The three women participants who have agreed to share excerpts from their longitudinal case reports have reviewed this manuscript and have consented to the publication of their case study data. George Santayana has written, "Nothing requires a rarer intellectual heroism than willingness to see one's equation written out." While this research project is still in process and the data base shared here represents only a glimpse of the whole, the willingness of each of them to provide a representative lens on her life events during this five year period is deeply appreciated, with respect and with affection. While each participant will recognize her own case study I have changed their names and the content focus

of some events to maintain their privacy. In doing this I
have carefully tried to fulfill my obligation to them without
making changes that would affect the developmental understanding of their cases.

My role as a case study researcher should also be put before you. It is an understatement to say that I have not conducted this study in a distanced, totally objective fashion. In
contrast, I co-taught the experimental class with the passion
of a feminist who was committed to helping the next generation of women seek meaning and choice in their lives.[2] And,
I believe I also helped them to realize that by committing
themselves to a study of women's lives in progress they have
made an important contribution to needed research on the
psychological constructs of women. We have met annually
over the five year period in my living room. In these gather-
ings the sense of re-union has always been with us—in the
personal bonds and in the unity of purpose. Since most of
the longitudinal participants still live near the university area,
there is an on-going exchange for many of us. We engage at
the corner drug store, walking by the river, riding the city
bus, buying books at the campus underground bookstore.
Two of the participants have worked as research assistants
for my colleagues, and one of these young women recently
shared her delight with me when she realized that the article
she was assigned in her psychology class was, in fact, a review
of the experimental curriculum for women in which she was
a participant. So, our lives are enmeshed and this psychological case study data must also be viewed from within this
anthropological framework.

In selecting case studies that would yield some new information about the experimental curriculum I research, I
decided to try to explore with you case reports on three
individuals whose measured outcomes on the intervention
instruments varied widely. Thus, Michele (Case #7, Appendix
A) showed pre- to post-intervention gains on both the ego
and moral instruments; Janet (Case #2, Appendix A) showed
pre- to post losses on both instruments over this intervention
period; and Joanne (Case #3, Appendix A) showed no

change on either instrument during the intervention nor during the first year follow-up study.

Some specific background information on these three women who have shared their case reports follows:

Michele: Michele is the fourth child in a family of six children. By 1973 records, her mother was not employed in addition to her home responsibilities. Her father is a prominent commercial artist and Michele lists her own career direction as "I am very interested in becoming an artist as my Dad is an artist and he likes it a lot and has encouraged me to start at it. Also, I would like to design clothes, and sew them and probably sell them." Michele reports (1973) she has worked as a secretarial aide, does routine housework in rotation with her family, and has been active in sports (capatain of a basketball team), and in contemporary dance and ballet. She reports that she has dated, but seldom.

Janet: Janet also has several siblings; she is the fifth child in a family of seven children. According to her 1973 data, her mother was employed as a clerk in an office and her father was a tradesman. In response to a question on career ideas she was considering, Janet replied, "Doctor, 'cause I want to be one." Janet (1973) has worked outside her home as a housecleaner and reports she has regular jobs in her home—cleaning and doing dishes. In response to questions on school activities and leadership roles she writes repeatedly, "I don't know." She reports (1973) she hadn't yet dated.

Joanne: Joanne is the oldest of two children in a family where (1973) the mother is a "freelance musician and teacher" and the father is a "freelance musician and college teacher." Joanne reports career ideas at that time as "Ethnomusicologist—I have music but can't play anything; historian—love ancient history since I learned it in 5th Grade; Bum—it's easier." She has worked as an usher at a theater, and does dishwashing, lawnmowing, and 'catbox cleaning' at her home. Joanne has been active in

FHA, urban arts dancing and orchestra, and a choir group. She checked a response (1973) that she did not date at all yet.

THREE CENTRAL THEMES IN DEVELOPMENTAL DATA: TIME, COMPLEXITY, SELF-ORGANIZATION

Case studies are always in process. But, at some point in time, cumulative reports can be woven together to catch a glimpse of the whole. We are studying the increasing complexity of human change across many facets, that occurs over time, which can result in increasingly adequate self-organization. It is interesting to note that these three interacting themes—time, complexity, and reorganization—seem to be the dominant themes which occur across all change processes, from transformations in microscopic crystals to movements of heavenly bodies in the Solar System.[3] I will try to examine these three themes through the lens of developmental theory and then make selected applications both to individual and to multiple case study data.

Time

Two concepts of time need to be placed before us in case study analysis: a) the impact of time in terms of historical context such that we recognize we are studying one life at one time in history; and b) time in the context of stage related structural change such that we recognize quantity of time as a necessary but not sufficient condition for tracking out invariant sequences in stage movement.

Time as Historical Context

Perhaps Erik Erikson has most successfully stressed the importance of historical context in the biography of a given life. His psychoanalytic studies of selected lives capture the constructive match of turbulent periods of history with particular psychic turbulences in his case studies.

Time, in terms of dissonance-producing historical context, can provide the initial triggering momentum for planned developmental interventions. Given this renaissance era of the women's rights movement, one would expect that those women who enrolled in the experimental class would have been self-selected for a high probability of change. Indeed, in checking back on the responses to a questionnaire given the first day of the experimental class, 19 of the 23 participants gave in reply to the question, "What are some reasons that influenced your decision to take this class?" statements that were related to the women's movement. Quotations from the three selected case reports on this question follow:

> *Michele*: "The description of (the) Women's Search for Identity class seemed to be interesting; different class. The class fitted in with my schedule. As I don't know much about Women's Lib, etc., I am interested in the subject. (Also) Mozey was teaching it."

> *Janet*: There wasn't anything else to take so I thought this might be interesting; by girl friend was taking it."

> *Joanne*: "I thought it sounded extremely interesting to learn about women's search for identity; I'm for women's (and people's) liberation and I wanted to learn more about women in literature."

Thus, Michele and Joanne responded to their interest in the women's movement. Janet, like the other three persons who gave no clear response that was related to the movement, gave functional and affiliation reasons.

In summary, most of the young women who enrolled in the 1973 experimental class gave some response indicating that their choice to participate was related to awareness of the women's rights movement. Time, in terms of historical context, has likely had a strong pull on their lives, for as Erik Erikson has written, "One cannot lift a case history out of history."

Given that historical context likely generated a dissonance that could lead to growth, can we in some way examine the power of the curriculum itself? Matched groups for controlling for the effects of the independent variables were not available. A time lag study for identifying historical effects was impractical. Given these limitations, the within group data gathered over five years was examined using a multiple regression analysis. A regression of the Kohlberg 1977 scores on the Kohlberg 1973 pre- and post-test intervention scores indicated that with the 1973 post-test scores, significantly more of the variance on the criterion 1977 scores was predicted than when the pre-test scores were used alone. During the 12-week intervention period something occurred which does improve the predictability of the 1977 moral judgment scores. A parallel test on the Loevinger/Wessler ego data does not give a multiple R that is significant on this more global construct. In the next section I will examine excerpts from the selected case studies which lend clinical evidence to the power of the intervention as experienced by the individual participant.

Time as a Necessary But Not Sufficient Condition for Developmental Growth:

While time, complexity, and self-organization are all enmeshed themes, specific aspects of the particular parameter of time can be set forth. The idea of designing educational interventions to deliberately promote structural change in the individual's thought processes has been referred to by Piaget as "The American Question." However, acceleration of structural complexity through planned intervention has been shown to occur for individuals participating in a class within time periods ranging from two weeks (Blasi, 1971) to the more typical 10-12 weeks (Erickson (Ed.), 1977).

While developmental stage attainment is age-related generally at least up to the conventional level, and while the movement from one stage to the next can be accelerated through interventions for some individuals, researchers do not yet know whether each individual has some minimal time requirement within a given stage that can't be modified by planned intervention. Also, stage regressions or developmental deflections are observed in data collected over time.

From my preliminary analysis of the data on the 21 case studies collected over the 12-week intervention and subsequent five year testing period, patterns between stage movements and the parameters of time can be observed (see Appendices A and B).

In studying Appendix A, it is evident that about two-thirds of the participants in the 12-week class showed an increase in moral judgment stage scores and about one-half of the participants had gains in ego stage scores, one person showed no stage score changes and six persons actually had decreases in their scores on at least one of the developmental measures from the pre- to post-testings. A closer look at this data is in order. Were optimal conditions for learning provided for some participants and not others? What differences exist in how persons in these groups report their 12-week intervention experience?

At this time of preliminary data analysis I will only speak to the general trends and then examine specific reports from the selected cases. For those participants who showed measured increases in their ego and moral stage attainment, a consistent pattern existed in their responses to the question: "What impact did the class have on you. . . .?" All of those with score increases made some reference to a change in their own thinking which they then attributed to particular units or exercises in the 12-week curriculum. As an example, Michele, who showed stage score gains on both the ego and moral measures, gave the following responses to this question over the five year study:

Michele

> 1974: "Before the Women's class I was not aware of the different options women are able to choose from . . . the class opened my eyes to the many alternatives of life which women have . . . The first day of the class each student was asked to tell a little about ourselves . . . This first day I was able to convey my thoughts to people who

seemed to care . . . this continued through the course . . .
I am more open with myself and people."

1975: "The most significant part of the Women's class
was the writing we did in our journals . . . little tangents
from my journal (still) pop up occasionally . . . I have
continued writing a journal for myself."

1976: "The freedom to express my feelings about myself
and towards different areas was first then experienced . . .
I have a journal which I've maintained for two years. The
Women's class initiated that interest in expressing myself
in words."

1977: "The Women's class came at a perfect time for me;
I was in the middle of changing my values . . . the journal
was very valuable to me, and having the guidance of the
idea or topic to write about . . . my writing was a new
step in seeing myself differently, more as a woman and
a person—since I have continued to write and share the
detailed parts of myself."

Thus, Michele, like others in this group, identified change
in her own thinking which she attributed to specific units in
the 12-week curriculum.

For those students in the sample who decreased in ego
or moral stage score during the 12-week period, consistent
themes in their responses to the probe question "What impact did the class have on you . . . ?" were a protective holding on to some particular belief or the experience of feeling
caught in the conflicting values of other persons. The responses of Janet (who decreased on both the ego and moral
measures) capture both of these themes and also give evidence to a shift in her reflections on the class over the five
year period.

Janet

1974: "It did affect me a little but I don't think that
mentally I was ready for it because all it did was mix me
up on things. Because I was being pulled from one side

by my family . . . and the other side by this class and all it did was mix me up . . . There really wasn't anything that 'stuck' with me because I was only taking this class for the English credit." (See her previous comments on her motivations for taking class.)

1975: "It didn't influence me at all; it did get me thinking about things but it didn't change it."

1976: "It didn't have that much impact on me but it did make me aware of the problems of women's rights."

1977: "It made me really think about what I wanted out of life and my rights. Also, the possibilities for my life . . . I find now keeping a journal helps me get things out of my system. Writing things down in class gave me the habit of writing things down when the class was over."

Thus, it appears that Janet experienced such dissonance during the 12-week course that rather than facilitate a new integration she states, "All it did was mix me up." For her, integration over time seemed to be needed to process the experience in a meaningful way.

Finally, Joanne is the one young woman who showed no measured change on the developmental instruments over the 12-week intervention, nor even one year later. She scored at a rather complex conscientious ego level (I-4) at those testings and at a typical Stage 3 conformity level in her moral reasoning. Of interest, in her clinical data her responses on the five year Annual Questionnaire to the probe: "What impact did the class have on you . . .?" reflect a somewhat detached series of observations of the other class participants. She herself confirms this in her 1977 statement when she discusses her feelings of being "different or separate."

Joanne

1974: "The class showed me that women were interested in changing or at least learning about their roles and exploring new possibilities."

1975: "I remember being pleasantly surprised that most of the people in the class didn't see themselves or their lives in the typical female stereotypes that I thought would be more common."

1976: "The Woman's class showed me that giggly, teenage girls in high school, who I had always looked at as a solid group with no real personality of their own, were people and very interesting women. It changed the way I looked at the rest of the girls."

1977: "The class showed me that other women my age were interested in themselves . . . and growing emotionally, not just in boys, clothes, and cliques; before the class I felt different or separate—the class showed me that more people felt the way I did than I had thought."

For Joanne, then, who at the onset of the class was one of the five participants measuring at a conscientious ego level, the curriculum over the 12-week period did not likely have the power to trigger measurable new thinking. The stability of her scores over the 1973-1974 year add evidence to this conclusion.

It should be noted that in the above excerpts of sequential data an increasing complexity and self-organization becomes evident.

The Theme of Increasing Complexity as Viewed from a Developmental Lens

When teaching adolescents, in particular, and when tracking out their young lives in progress, we are continually identifying new evidence of their emerging complexity of thought. Piaget has empirically researched how the onset of formal operational thought in the adolescent equips her/him with the capacity for more adequate conceptualization. Kohlberg and Loevinger, respectively, acknowledge the transformation to formal operational thought as a necessary (not not sufficient) condition for reaching the postconventional moral and ego stages. Loevinger (1976, p. 23) states that, "Conceptual complexity is an outstanding sign of both the autonomous and the integrated (ego) stages." Thus, for adolescents who are shifting from conventional modes of thought, there is a beginning of the transcending of polarities and a recognition of reality as being complex and multifaceted; there is a new uniting and integrating of ideas that appeared as incompatible alternatives at lower stages. This increasing complexity makes possible new interactions with the world. The adolescents' conceptions of self, others, and society can become more differentiated; their understanding of morality can become more adequate. Through this increased complexity a new self-organization can also emerge which offers a more coherent inner logic for seeking forms and order.

To try to track out this growth process in complexity through case study examples is not a process which is easily reportable. From my beginning analyses, it seems that by getting a good grasp of multiple growth theories; by seeking and valuing an extensive, in-depth exposure to the participants; by reading the works of colleagues who have tried to bridge theory with practice, and then by letting it all re-intergrate—again and again, the developmental stage framework seems to emerge as an enlightening backdrop to the uniqueness of the individual case study. In sorting out the myriad of five year data gathered in this research study, I've tried to find examples of sequential data excerpts which capture this increased complexity. I have traced this theme across journal pages, across annual questionnaire responses, and across the annual responses of selected developmental instruments. For the purposes and space of this chapter, I've tried to find representative excerpts that would offer a glimpse of increased complexity within the same content area. To do this, I have chosen sentence stems from the Loevinger/Wessler Sentence Completion Test (SCT). I will present a selected stem, across five year data, for each case report. It needs to be recognized that only the SCT taken as a whole (36 stems) is researched to represent a measure of ego structure. However, by selecting individual stems and tracking out a response of a given content over several years, the theme of increasing complexity as a clue to the developing ego stage can be demonstrated. The SCT directions to the 36 stems which are spread over three standardized typing sheets are: "Complete the following sentences in any way that you wish."

Michele's responses to the Sentence Stem:
Most men think that women . . . .

1973 pre: are just an object.

1974 post: are not very intelligent.

1974: are sex objects.

1975: are incapable of many things, but little do many men realize a woman's capacity—emotionally, physically.

1976: are only meant to be a play object to fulfill men's desires.

1977: are not as deeply capable emotionally, physically, intellectually and spiritually as is actually true with many women.

Janet's responses to the Sentence Stem:
If my mother . . . .

1973 pre: wanted me to do something I'd usually do it.

1973 post: (omitted)

1974: liked to have fun more I probably would like her better.

1975: was like me her life would be totally different.

1976: were me I might be a better person.

1977: could understand me better she would know why I am like I am.

Joanne's responses to the Sentence Stem:
Rules are . . . .

1973 pre: too unflexible.

1973 post: sometimes good, but often they don't meet the needs of many.

    1974: necessary in moderation, but absurd when you don't understand the reason for rules, or when there's too many.

    1975: made to be broken, bent, or changed, but they are necessary in this society.

    1976: usually hard to accept for me, if I'm not the one to make them; but sometimes it's easier to fall back on rules rather than being honest.

    1977: necessary in today's society, but should be constantly open to change and revision.

A shift toward increased complexity is evident in all of the above response sequences. Over the five years, Joanne responded with increased awareness of exceptions and contingencies, she came to see rules within a societal context, and she understood inherent contradictions. Michele's quotations are taken from a stem which pulls for conformity responses to men's perceptions of women. She transcended this over time to express awareness of the stereotype in its multifaceted forms, evaluated it from a distance, then negated its truth for many women. The responses of Janet to the "If my mother . . . ." stem also moved from a conformity response to greater differentiation. She progressed by focusing on her relationship with her mother, then she indicated a conscientious level identification of herself with her mother, and in her last response showed some evidence of distancing, and viewing the relationship in the context of two interacting separate persons.

The successions of increasing complexity of thought, interpersonal relationships, moral character, and psychological causation have been set forth by Loevinger (1976) as facets of a single process, ego development. The successive stages of structural unity or self-organization will be reviewed within the case study methodology in the next section.

The Theme of Increasing Adequacy
of Self-Organization in Developmental Case Study Data

The development of self-organization, or ego as defined by Loevinger (1976), and the subset structure of moral character as defined by Kohlberg (1969) can be mapped out in this study through the annual data collected over five years (Appendix A), and by thematic analyses of journals and questionnaire responses. In this section I will discuss preliminary analyses of data trends on the instruments; I will identify some major shifts occurring across the data and share with you a methodology for identifying concomitants of change; I will then set forth some of the reported concomitants of change occurring in the lives of the three selected participants, and will also present brief excerpts from their case reports which offer a glimpse of their own conceptions of their own self-organization.

In examining the ego data (Appendix B) for general trends across the 21 participants over five years, it is evident that: a) during middle adolescence and through the high school years, ego level tends to increase steadily; and b) as with all growth curves, tapering off occurs with maturity, in this sample with the conclusion of high school. The mean ego level shifted from a conscientious conformist (I-3/4) for the sample as high school sophomores to a conscientious level (I-4) at the close of their senior year in high school, stabilizing there over the next two years. Test-retest correlations across the five year ego data show positive correlations for every pair (range= .5 -.7), all significantly different from zero. Of importance, the group as a whole emerged five years later in the study with a mean ego level higher than that expected in the general population, and six of the 21 participants have a pattern of individualistic (I-4/5) ego level or higher.

The moral judgment data on the 21 women also show developmental growth across the five year study; however, with some deflections occurring in the participants' senior year testing. While the mean moral maturity score indicates about a 1/3 stage positive movement (34 points) over the five year testing span, the shift in moral judgment stage scores is more indicative of structural transformation. In the 1973 pre-testing only three participants held some Stage 4 moral reasoning while eight students still had some Stage 2 responses in their reasoning. By 1977, 14 students showed some Stage 4 moral reasoning and only two young women had Stage 2 reasoning in their protocols. Test-retest correlations across the five year Moral Maturity Scores show positive correlations for every pair, four of the five years significant from zero (range= .3-.9; the two extreme correlations in this range reflect the drop of eight participants' scores in the 1975 testing and a problem of incomplete data in 1979, such that four test results from the previous year had to be used).

It is of particular interest in examining this data that Stage 3 conformity thinking persists in the scores of all 21 women during the five year period. Even among those six participants who scored I-4/5 or higher on the ego measure, all six maintained at least a minor Stage 3 in their moral stage scores. As discussed elsewhere (Erickson, Gibbs, Berkowitz, in preparation) this plateauing may reflect sex role socialization, scoring limitations, interpretations of Piagetian structrual stages, or a combination of these factors.

In this chapter the weaving of individual case study data into the general findings has been presented as a beginning attempt to expand upon the data and to gain some new understandings. At this time in my overall analysis of the case studies I am in a preliminary stage of systematically sorting, arranging, and examining the five year data to hypothesize concomitants of change. Thus, I am trying to identify combinations of variables that seem to have impacted participants of this study in a particular way. I am asking the question, "What reported life experiences at given stages of development are associated with developmental growth, plateauing of growth, or to a decline in growth (as measured by the Kohlberg and Loevinger instruments) in this study of 21 young women over five years?"

The following method of sorting, arranging, and examining the data provides a means of bridging empirical data with case study reports such that measured structural change can be related to reported life experiences (the Norem-Habeisen, Erickson article reference details this process and it can be obtained from this author).

Methodology for Identifying Concomitants of Change Across Developmental Case Studies

1. The protocols are first sorted into groups on the basis of marked change computed in each instrument for each participant.

2. The protocols are then reviewed by group and basic themes common to all protocols in the group are identified. (Themes have included such variables as active pursuit of new experiences, assertions for meeting one's own needs, success or failure in new experience and self-assertions, stress experienced, degrees of stress, coping responses of confrontation or avoidance, positive and negative outcomes of coping responses.)

3. Explicit definitions are then established for each theme.

4. The protocols are then reviewed again by two raters who negotiate inconsistencies in identified themes.

5. The number and category of each theme present in each of the participants' protocols is then tallied.

6. A chart is prepared which summarizes and collates the interview data with the indices of marked gain, loss, or no change on the instruments.

7. The participants are then arranged into groupings on the basis of marked change scores across instruments.

8. Patterns of relationships between the change scores and the themes presented in their reports are then identified.

9. Hypotheses on concomitants for change are then generated.

Reported Life Experiences and Structural Shifts
in the Three Selected Case Studies

Some obvious data shifts in the sequential ego and moral scores of Joanne, Michele, and Janet (Appendix A) reflect their reported life events at those developmental moments.

For Joanne, who had stabilized at a conscientious ego stage and a conformity stage of moral judgment over the first three testings, it is important to observe that in the 1975 testing both her ego and moral judgment scores show a developmental increase. Her succeeding test scores then again stabilize. What reported experiences might have triggered the measured growth? Some excerpts from Joanne's self reports indicated a major shift occurred for her when she left high school. (Note: She completed high school mid-year in her senior year.)

Joanne

> 1975: "I've really been growing up in this year. I'm out of high school, taking one class at the U of M which gives me a sense of more independence—I'm separated from lots of my friends, and people my age, and I get sort of lonely sometimes . . . ."

> 1976: "The most important thing that has happened to me in the last three years was getting out of high school. As I look back on high school, I realize that life there was very removed from 'the real world.' I've learned more about just surviving and getting along with myself in the last 1-1/2 years than I did in six years of high school . . . ."

For Janet, the mismatch of the curriculum to the combination of her developmental stage and her family's values, as quoted from her earlier, provide the background data for her first developmental deflection. She then regains her ego and moral stage scores in 1974 (both at Stage 3). Her 1975 data then presents new questions. While her ego score reflects an increase in complexity and adequacy (I-3/4), she shows an unexpected minor stage in her moral judgment 3(1). My first thoughts in reviewing the data was that this must be a scoring error. I went to the clinical self-report data for the year and found that Janet had not completed the sections on life experiences. In the following years, 1976 and 1977, Janet's ego scores were maintained at a stable I-3/4 and her moral judgment scores increased to a 3/4. I will quote from her poignant self-report at these testing times to share her reported life experiences. They seem to confirm the inherent strength of her own ego and also offer construct validity to the Kohlberg measure.

Janet

> 1976: "Since 1973 I have had a lot happen to me. I had my first boyfriend. That experience was good and bad. As I look back I remember finding out what jealousy was and also what love and a broken heart felt like. I also got pregnant without being married . . . I went through a very depressing time wondering 'should I keep the baby, should I give it up, or should I have an abortion?' Well, abortion was out so I decided to keep the baby. I also wondered if the father would marry me. Well, it turns out he didn't. Now I am spending my days with a beautiful baby girl and I think it's the most rewarding thing I've ever done in my whole life and I wish I didn't have to work."

> 1977: ". . . I had a child and found the patience and love that only a child can give you. I found a man that lets me be what I want to be and loves me for what I am."

Rest (1974, p. 245) writes that ". . . the essential condition for the cumulative elaboration of cognitive structure is the presentation of experiences which 'stretch' one's existing thinking and set into motion this search-and-discovery process for more adequate ways to organize experience and action." The reported life experiences and reflections of Michele over her five year data seem to clinically validate how the stretch-and-discovery process for her led to continual developmental growth.

Michele

1975: "The last two years in Colorado (boarding school her junior and senior years) have been incredibly important and worthwhile. I have changed in many ways . . . most significantly in that I have realized much about myself, my life, my past . . . living isn't as pleasant as I had envisioned and not as easy either . . . through people and experiences I have become more aware of my short-comings and my good points also. And, from these I am left . . . trying to understand and question who I am, what I am, and why . . . ."

1977: "Moving away from home to attend a boarding school was a major change, away from the securities and dependencies of home . . . graduating from high school—into the big world. No college ahead of me, 'What do I do now?' syndrome. Saw a psychiatrist during an intense time of family problems and growth. Uncomfortable time. Move to San Francisco. My own freedom. Supporting myself financially . . . new friends . . . actualization workshops . . . much acknowledgment from older friends. Men started to become more comfortable and fun in my life. Moved to Madison . . . was not committed to school aspect . . . back to San Francisco to settle myself down. From all these changes and experiences I've grown to where I am now . . . a time for much reflection. . . analysis of myself and a look at goals . . . ."

In closing, it is my hope that this chapter has presented a more in-depth, complex, wholistic, yet differentiated account of ". . . what actually takes place when education really occurs." I again express my deep gratitude to the three participants who have shared excerpts from their own lives in progress.

APPENDIX A

Table 1

The Patterning of Loevinger Ego Scores and Kohlberg Moral Judgment Scores of 21 Young Women Over a Five-Year Period

Code #	6/73 Age	PRE 1973	POST (3 Month Intervention)	1974	1975	1976	1977
1	15-10	I-4 (337) 3(4)	I-4/5 378 4(3)	I-4/5 363 4(3)	I-4/5 343 3(4)	I-4/5 375 4(3)	I-4 368 4(3) Use 1976 Kohlberg Data
2	15-5	I-3 (283) 3	I-2 217 2(3)	I-3 294 3	I-3/4 209 3(1)	I-3/4 350 3/4	I-3/4 Use 1976 Kohlberg Data
3	15-2	I-4 318 3	I-4 (319) 3	I-4 (309) 3	I-4/5 341 3(4)	I-4/5 (347) 3(4)	I-4/5 (325) 3(4)
4	15-0	I-3 290 3	I-3/4 (225) 2(3)	I-3/4 (265) 3(2)	I-3/4 (259) 3(4)	I-3/4 (267) 3(2)	I-3 (260) 3(2)
5	16-4	I-3 (293) 3	I-3/4 300 3	I-3/4 295 3	I-4 329 3(4)	I-3/4 300 3	I-3/4 314 3
6	16-6	I-3/4 (273) 3(2)	I-3/4 317 3	I-3/4 300 3	I-4 310 3	I-4 300 3	I-4 300 3
7	16-0	I-3/4 279 3(2)	I-4 (300) 3	I-4 (317) 3	I-4/5 (300) 3	I-5 (377) 4(3)	I-5 (359) 4(3)
8	15-10	I-3/4 265 3(2)	I-3/4 (350) 3/4	I-4 (340) 3(4)	I-3/4 (319) 3	Use 1975 Data	I-3/4 (350) 3/4
9	15-4	I-3/4 256 3(2)	I-4 (268) 2(3)	I-4 (335) 3(4)	I-3/4 (322) 3(4)	I-3/4 (332) 3(4)	I-3/4 (334) 3(4)
10	15-6	I-3/4 (333) 3/4	I-3/4 376 4(3)	I-4 377 3/4	I-4 314 3	I-4 388 4(3)	I-4 359 4(3)
11	15-9	I-4 (278) 3(2)	I-4/5 345 3(4)	I-4/5 354 4(3)	I-4/5 325 3(4)	I-4 308 3	Use 1976 Data
12	16-4	I-3/4 (308) 3	I-4 337 3(4)	I-3/4 323 3(4)	I-4 350 3/4	I-4 325 3(4)	I-4 323 3(4)
13	16-1	I-4 (277) 3	I-4 338 3(4)	I-4 336 3(4)	I-4 300 3	I-4/5 305 3	I-4 329 3(4)
14	15-7	I-4 300 3	I-4 (250) 2/3	I-3/4 (225) 2	I-4 (281) 3(2)	I-4 310 3	I-3/4 (262) 3(2)
15	15-6	I-3 (243) 2(3)	I-3 300 3	I-3 317 3	I-3/4 291 3	I-3/4 310 3	I-4 325 3(4)
16	15-8	I-4 (317) 3	I-3 (330) 3(4)	I-3/4 332 3(4)	I-4 250 2(3)(4)	I-3/4 305 3	I-3/4 331 3(4)
17	15-8	I-3/4 (319) 3	I-4 320 3(4)	I-4 321 3(4)	I-4 319 3	I-3/4 357 4(3)	I-4/5 334 3(4)
18		259 3(2)	(194) 2				
19	16-1	I-3/4 (353) 4(3)	I-3/4 327 3(4)	I-4 300 3	I-4/5 341 3(4)	I-4/5 338 3(4)	I-4 350 3/4
20	16-3	I-3/4 296 3	I-4 (333) 3(4)	I-4 (333) 3(4)	I-4 (320) 3(4)	I-4 (338) 3(4)	Use 1976 Data
21	16-6	I-3 270 3(2)	I-3/4 (313) 3	I-3/4 (305) 3	I-3/4 (289) 3	I-4 (310) 3	I-3/4 (315) 3
22	16-1	I-3/4 (254) 3(2)	I-4 286 3	I-4/5 335 3(4)	I-4 333 3(4)	I-4/5 314 3	I-4/5 Use 1976 Kohlberg Data
23		300(2)3(4)	200 2				

–Scores in horizontal order: Ego Stage Score, Moral Maturity Score, Moral Stage Score.
–Kohlberg Moral Maturity Scores on Form C are bracketed ( ). Form A Scores are without brackets.
–Tests in 1973, 1974 were administered in group settings, written forms;
  the written forms were distributed by mail to participants in years 1975, 1976, 1977.
–Prior year data is used when individual has missed a testing or responses on the
  Kohlberg Interview are insufficient for scoring (N=5 total).

Appendix B

Mean Loevinger Ego Score by Year in a Sample of 21 Young Women

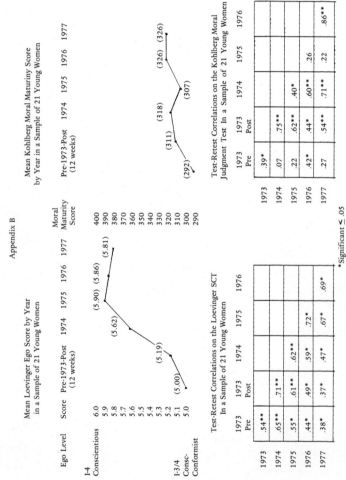

Ego Level	Score	Pre-1973-Post (12 weeks)	1974	1975	1976	1977
I-4 Conscientious	6.0				(5.90) (5.86)	(5.81)
	5.9					
	5.8					
	5.7					
	5.6					
	5.5			(5.62)		
	5.4					
	5.3					
	5.2	(5.19)				
I-3/4 Consc-Conformist	5.1					
	5.0	(5.00)				

Mean Kohlberg Moral Maturiny Score by Year in a Sample of 21 Young Women

	Moral Maturity Score	Pre-1973-Post (12 weeks)	1974	1975	1976	1977
	400					
	390					
	380					
	370					
	360					
	350					
	340					
	330			(318)	(326)	(326)
	320	(311)				
	310			(307)		
	300	(292)				
	290					

Test-Retest Correlations on the Loevinger SCT In a Sample of 21 Young Women

	1973 Pre	1973 Post	1974	1975	1976
1973	.54**				
1974	.65**	.71**			
1975	.55*	.61**	.62**		
1976	.44*	.49*	.59*	.72*	
1977	.38*	.37*	.47*	.67*	.69*

Test-Retest Correlations on the Kohlberg Moral Judgment Test In a Sample of 21 Young Women

	1973 Pre	1973 Post	1974	1975	1976
1973	.39*				
1974	.07	.75**			
1975	.22	.62**	.40*		
1976	.42*	.44*	.60**	.26	
1977	.27	.54**	.71**	.22	.86**

*Significant ≤ .05
**Significant ≤ .01

REFERENCE NOTES

1. My appreciation is extended to John Gibbs, Anne Colbly, Betsy Speicher-Dubin, and Lawrence Kohlberg for their extensive work on the scoring and their suggestions for analysis of the five year moral judgment data. I also want to extend my thanks to Joshua Martin for his scoring of the five year Loevinger data.

2. The course was team-taught with Mary Mozey; Charlotte Rogers and Barbara Glaser-Kirshenbaum also taught specific units. My appreciation is extended to each of them.

3. See the works of Ilya Prigogine on dissapative structures. (**From Being to Becoming**, in press with W. H. Freeman Co., San Francisco.)

4. Carol Gilligan (Harvard University) has developed an extensive questionnaire probing the construct of the ego. Her questions were included in the 1976 and 1977 data collections in this study.

REFERENCES

Block, J. **Lives Through Time**. Berkeley, California: Bancroft Books, 1971.

Blasi, G. In J. Loevinger (Ed.), **Ego Development**. San Francisco: Jossey-Bass, 1976.

Bolgar, H. "The Case Study Method." In B. Wolman (Ed.), **Handbook of Clinical Psychology**. New York: McGraw-Hill, 1965.

Dukes, W. F. "N=1." *Psychological Bulletin*, 1965, 64, 74-79.

Erickson, V. L. (Ed.), *The Counseling Psychologist*, Vol. 6, #4, 1977a.

Erickson, V. L. *Moral Education Forum*, Vol. II, #4, September, 1977b.

Erickson, V. L., Gibbs, J. C., and Berkowitz, M. W. "Sex Differences in Moral Judgment During Adolexcence and Young Adulthood," paper in preparation.

Erikson, E. **Young Man Luther**. New York: W. W. Norton and Company, 1958.

Erikson, E. **Ghandi's Truth**. New York: W. W. Norton and Company, 1969.

Freud, S. **New Introductory Lectures on Psychoanalysis**. New York: W. W. Norton and Company, 1933.

Gibbs, J. C. "The Meaning of Ecologically Oriented Inquiry in Contemporary Psychology." *American Psychologist*, Vol. 34, #2, February, 1979.

Harre, R., and Secord, P. F. **The Explanation of Social Behavior.** Totowa, New Jersey: Littlefield, Adams, and Col., 1972.

Houser, S. T. "Loevinger's Model and Measure of Ego Development: A Critical Review." *Psychological Bulletin*, 1976, 88, 5.

Kohlberg, L. "Stage and Sequence: The Cognitive-Developmental Approach to Socialization." In D. Goslin (Ed.), **Handbook of Socialization Theory and Research.** Chicago: Rand McNally, 1969, 347-480.

Kounin, J. S. "An Ecological Approach to Classroom Activity Settings: Some Methods and Findings." In R. A. Weinberg and F. A. Woods (Eds.), **Observation of Pupils and Teachers in Mainstream and Special Education Settings: Alternative Stretegies.** Minneapolis, Minnesota: Leadership Training Institute/Special Education, 1975, 9-40.

Kratochwill, T. (Ed.), **Single Subject Research: Strategies for Evaluating Change.** Academic Press, 1978.

Loevinger, J. **Ego Development.** San Francisco: Jossey-Bass, 1976.

Norem-Hebeisen, A. A., and Erickson, V. L. "Women's Development: Concomitants of Growth." Submitted for publication, 1980.

Riegel, K. "The Dialectics of Human Development." *American Psychologist*, October, 1976, 689-700.

Rest, J. "Developmental Psychology as a Guide to Value Education: A Review of 'Kohlbergian' Programs." *Review of Educational Research*, 1974, 44, (2), 241-259.

Shine, L. C. "Five Research Steps Designed to Integrate the Single Subject and Multi-Subject Approaches to Experimental Research." *Canadian Psychological Review*, 1975, 23, 643-652.

Stake, R. E. "The Case Study Method in Social Inquiry." *Educational Researcher*, February, 1978.

White, R. W. **Lives in Progress.** New York: Holt, Rinehart, and Winston, 1952.

Witherell, C. E., and Erickson, V. L. "Teacher Education as Adult Development: A Perspective from Ego Psychology." In *Theory Into Practice*, Vol. XVIII, #3, June, 1978, 229-238.

Chapter 13

EVALUATING JUST COMMUNITIES:
TOWARD A METHOD FOR ASSESSING
THE MORAL ATMOSPHERE OF THE SCHOOL

Clark Power

In 1897 John Dewey (1897/1959) offered the following critique of the dominant practice of education at that time:

> I believe that much of present education fails because it neglects this fundamental principle of the school as a form of community life. It conceives the school as a place where certain information is to be given, where certain lessons are to be learned, or where certain habits are to be formed . . . .
> I believe that the moral education centers upon this conception of the school as a mode of social life, that the best and deepest moral training is precisely that which one gets through having to enter into proper relations with others in a unity of work and thought. The present educational systems, so far as they destroy or neglect this unity, render it difficult or impossible to get any genuine, regular moral training. (Dewey, pp. 23-24)

What was true for the close of the 19th century appears equally true for today. Educators tend to think of schools as institutions offering a wide range of services but not as cooperative communities. In order to provide the best possible facilities (e.g., science labs, libraries, and gymnasiums) and highly specialized curricula, larger schools have been built and educators have narrowly focused on training individuals to take up functional roles in the technopolis. The price which our society now appears to be paying for the trend is the disinterest and alienation of its youth.

THE JUST COMMUNITY APPROACH
TO MORAL EDUCATION

Kohlberg (in press) has reasserted the Deweyian position on building community in the school. His educational theory, termed "The Just Community Approach," prescribes the use of democratic procedures and emphasizes the importance of focusing the attention of staff and students on matters of fairness and community. Kohlberg sees democratic community as a means and an end of moral education.

As a means he claims that community promotes the kinds of social interactions and relationships conducive to individual moral development. Participating in a genuine educational community provides a concentrated opportunity for students and teachers to explore the dynamics of social relationships, to cooperate in the learning process, and to resolve social conflicts openly and equitably. In thinking about the just community approach as an educational means, we must be careful not to adopt an instrumental view of community as deriving its value solely in terms of what it can contribute to individual stage development. Building a just community is also an educational end. As Kohlberg argues, we must acknowledge that the building of a just community is inherently worthwhile and should thus be considered as an educational goal.

Partly as a response to the neglect of this principle of community in the mainstream of American education, concerned educators and parents have established a number of "Alternative Schools." In these schools they have experimented with various forms of governance, discipline, and curricula in order to stimulate student interest and initiative in learning and to encourage greater equality in the relationships between students and faculty. By and large these schools have provided opportunities for students and teachers to jointly participate in decision-making, leading to the emergence of a sense of shared responsibility.

While many educators in these alternative schools recognize that building community is an important way of "humanizing" education, few have articulated the role of community within a theory of moral education. Thus when the Cluster School in Cambridge, Massachusetts, the School-Within-A-School in Brookline, Massachusetts, and the Scarsdale Alternative School in Scarsdale, New York explicitly decided to link community to a program of developmental moral education, a crucial experiment was set in motion. These schools aligned themselves with noted theorists and researchers in moral education—Kohlberg, Mosher, and Fenton—in an effort not only to improve their own programs but to become models for other schools.

Problems of Evaluating the Just Community Approach

The task of evaluating these schools has demanded the creation of a method of investigating the nature of their communities. I would like to outline some of the critical problems which those of us developing this new methodology have had to address and how these problems differ from those which researchers utilizing various formats of the Hypothetical Moral Judgment Interview have addressed. The first challenge we faced in evaluating these programs was to find a way of describing the moral characteristics of the community *qua* community; that is, the community as a social whole, distinct from the aggregate of individuals who compose it. This entailed a shift in perspective from a psychology of individual moral judgment to a sociology of shared norms and values. The Moral Judgment Interview helped to define those psychological structures which organize and guide individual reasoning and decision-making. There was a need for a complementary assessment technique which could help to define those normative group structures which provide cohesiveness and direction for the group.

Another problem arose out of the complexity of studying "real-life" behavior in a naturalistic setting. The Hypothetical

Moral Judgment Interview aptly controlled for such "extra-neous" influences on moral reasoning as familiarity with the characters in the dilemma, knowledge of the particular social institutions in which the dilemma occurs, and the pressures of having to act on whatever decision is chosen. Yet precisely these "extraneous" factors were of vital in-terest in evaluating particular schools. The transition from assessing moral competence to moral performance required the sacrifice of many of those "laboratory-like" conditions which made Kohlberg's original structural developmental analysis possible. The new methodology had to be flexible in utilizing all sources of information available about a particular program in order to interpret the meaning of particular events, statements, decisions, and actions. As evaluators we had to become not only pre- and post-test interviewers but participant observers of school functioning and historians charting the progress or decline of the com-munity.

Assessing Individual Development

In gathering data about Cluster, School-Within-A-School and Scarsdale Alternative School, we had two major ob-jectives. First, we wished to determine the impact of these schools on individual moral development. Second, we wished to describe the extent to which these schools became just communities. We had, of course, a measure of individual moral judgment development—the standard interview used in Kohlberg's longitudinal research. However, we felt we needed an additional measure of individual moral judgment which related specifically to problems students faced in the actual school setting. We were also interested in the way in which individual students appropriated the ideology of democratic community expounded by these schools. Therefore, we developed interview questions which asked students for their opinions about issues in the school and for their ideals of school democracy community, fairness and discipline (order).

Defining the Moral Atmosphere of the School

Collecting data about the just community required significant conceptual clarification about the phenomenon which
we wished to study. The major difficulty in evaluating just
community schools is finding appropriate categories and
methods which can aid in describing and assessing the "moral"
dimension of their community life. What distinguishes these
schools from others is the priority which their staff have
given to the creation of a social atmosphere which is both
just and communal. We use the term "moral atmosphere"
to refer to the moral quality of the collective norms and
valuing attitudes which characterize a social group.

In order to delineate more carefully what we mean by a
moral atmosphere, it is helpful to distinguish as does Moos
(1979) four different parts of the environmental system:
the physical setting, organizational factors, the human aggregate, and social atmosphere or climate. The physical setting
refers to architectural and physical design of school buildings
and classrooms which can have an influence on attitudes and
behavior. Organizational factors are "fixed" program components such as the size of the school, faculty-student ration,
form of governance, method of instruction (e.g., team teaching), etc. The human aggregate defines the characteristics of
the individuals making up the organization, for example, age,
SDS, IQ, stage of moral judgment, etc. The social atmosphere
actually arises out of the first three parts of the environmental system and mediates to some degree their influence.
But the social atmosphere cannot be reduced to the other
parts of the social system because it is created through the
interactions of the human aggregate as influenced by organizational factors in a particular physical setting. As such, a
social atmosphere must be conceptualized as distinct from
the other more stable parts of the environmental system.

There were two major studies of the moral atmosphere
of institutions by Scharf (1973) and by Reimer (1977) which
greatly influenced our research on these schools. Both focused
on the interaction between a particular environment and an

individual's stage of moral reasoning. Scharf (1973) found that the custodial prison environment had a negative effect on inmates' moral reasoning. Inmates tended to use a pre-conventional stage of moral judgment to reason about problems occurring in the prison situation even when they were capable of higher stage reasoning. On the other hand, Reimer (1977) found that the kibbutz environment had a positive effect on members' reasoning. Those who entered the kibbutz at a preconventional stage of reasoning experienced a great amount of conflict with kibbutz norms and soon developed to a conventional stage of reasoning. Scharf and Reimer demonstrated the powerful effect that an environment could have on an individual's moral reasoning. They left for our research the task of designing methods for a systematic description of the moral atmosphere of environments.

Community Meeting and Interview Analyses

We began constructing a method for assessing the moral atmosphere of schools by analyzing transcripts of Cluster community meetings (Power, 1978). The Cluster community meeting resembled a New England Town Meeting. All members of the school, staff and students, met once a week to discuss and to democratically make decisions relevant to the functioning of the school. The community meeting was the single most important activity for the building and mainte-nance of the Cluster community. Community meeting tran-scripts provided a rich source of information about how a moral atmosphere was promoted and maintained because it was in the community meeting that problems which affected the group were made public, discussed, and to some extent resolved.

The analysis of community meeting data is limited by the researchers' inability to probe statements as they are made and by the small percentage of students who actually speak up at a meeting. The community meeting analysis did, how-ever, lead to the development of a basic framework through an analysis of interviews, designed to probe for individual reactions to the events discussed in community meetings. We constructed two types of moral atmosphere interviews. In the first, the Ethnographic Interview, we asked students to review the crucial events and meetings which took place during the year and to give their impressions of what shared understandings, resolutions, and actions resulted. In the second, the School Dilemmas Interview, we asked students to respond to a series of dilemmas which typically occurred in their school. In addition to probing their personal resolutions of the dilemmas, we asked them to become spokespersons for the group and to represent the group's norms and values.

Conceptual Framework for Moral Atmosphere Assessment

In seeking a framework for analyzing statements made in community meetings and interviews, we borrowed from Kohlberg's Standard Moral Judgment Scoring Manual (Kohlberg, Colby, Gibbs, Speicher-Dubin, Power, and Candee, 1978), a way of dividing a morally prescriptive statement into two parts: the norm (*what* is being prescribed, e.g., trust, respect for property) and the element (*why* this is being prescribed, e.g., because it is fair to all involved, it will build community). These two parts correspond to two of Durkheim's elements of morality, the spirit of discipline and the spirit of altruism or attachment to the group.

A *norm*, as it is used in the Moral Judgment Scoring Manual, is actually a complex of specific behavioral expectations which share a common value. That value provides the motivation for upholding these expectations. For example, the norm of trust may be broken down behaviorally to mean: one should be able to share one's private possessions with others; one should not violate private possessions which have been left unguarded; and one should safeguard the possessions that others have left unguarded. Taken separately or together these norms lack an important motivational or valuing component which gives them meaning. Trust entails a concern for a relatedness to others which goes beyond specific actions. An *element* is a further justification of a norm which denotes its terminal value. For example, the obligation to trust may be based on the consideration that trust promotes harmony between individuals, which is a necessary condition for any social interaction.

An analysis of prescriptive statements according to the above framework aids us in assessing individuals' moral reasoning in a group context, but what can it tell us about the group itself? In order to answer this question we must determine whether the norms and elements which individuals express are shared by others in the group as common obligations or whether they are held individually. Of course, in analyzing the statements of any individual we only know what that individual thinks the collective obligations are. We still do not know to what extent group members agree on their perceptions of the collective norms and elements. However, before proceeding to ascertain the level of agreement among individuals in the group, it is necessary to identify those statements which refer to the group's collective norms and elements.

COLLECTIVE NORMS

The central unit in our analysis is the collective norm. We define a collective norm as a norm which binds members of a group *qua* group membership. A collective norm is a prescription for action; it defines *what is expected* from members in their attitudes (e.g., caring about the group) and actions (e.g., not stealing from others). It is important to note that we refer to a norm as an ideal or prescription for action and thus derive collective norms from what people state is expected in the group. We do not derive collective norms exclusively from inferences about actions. As an expectation, a collective norm has three characterisitics. First, it represents the "general will" or the shared expectation of the group as a whole, for example, "we, as a group, expect trust." Second, it defines an obligation which comes from group membership. Individuals are bound to uphold certain norms because they belong to a particular group and not simply because they are moral agents or have certain personal beliefs. Third, it arises out of the interactions of group members who seek to clarify what their responsibilities to each other and to the group should be. Thus in order to have a collective norm there must be some form of agreement among group members.

Within the general class of collective norms we were particularly interested in those norms which uphold the intrinsic value of community; that is, they are directed towards building the harmony of the group as a community. Collective norms of community value relationships of individual to individual, individual to group, and group to individual for their own sake. What is essential to all of these norms is that they prescribe sharing among members. Let me illustrate these prescriptions: *caring* implies sharing concerns and affection; *trust*, sharing one's confidence and property; *integration*, sharing of communication between subgroups; *participation*, sharing time, energy and interest; *publicity*, sharing knowledge about matters which affect the group. and *collective responsibility*, sharing obligations and fault.

In expressing collective norms individuals believe that they are representing the concerns of the whole group. However, there are two senses in which one may speak for a group: in an implicit, ideal sense and in an explicit, actual sense. In an implicit, ideal sense, the speaker knows that other members of the group do not (yet) explicitly share the value or norm. However, the speaker believes they ought to share the norm explicitly because it is implied by ideals of the group. Thus the speaker proposes collective norms for the group to accept. For example, in one of the community meeting discussions concerning stealing, a staff member spoke out:

> I think the issue is that the ripping off is not an individual business, it is community business . . . It is not as much a discipline issue as much as it is some feeling by the community that people have to have some level of trust.

He advocated a norm of trust because he thought trust was implied by the group's ideal of community, although he realized that the group did not yet explicityly share that norm. In an explicit, actual sense, the speaker thinks that other members do share the norm, for example, in a later meeting a student said, "Everyone here knows that we are supposed to trust each other."

Obviously, a collective norm which is being proposed by an individual is far less an attribute of a collectivity than a collective norm which is explicitly accepted and enforced. Thus we found it necessary to differentiate the varying degrees to which norms were collective through a scheme of phases (see Table 1).

The Phase of the Collective Norm

The scheme of phases traces a sequence in which norms become institutionalized in a group. Groups begin when individuals come together to pursue common goals and objectives. In the course of this coming together they make agreements which regulate their intentions and form shared ideals about the kind of group they wish to have. These agreements and shared ideals serve to organize the group and keep it whole and cohesive. Without them the group would fragment and cease to be. In a democracy agreements are made through a process of negotiation about what the duties of group membership entail. In order for these agreements to be effective, they must be upheld by members of the group. Otherwise, they will have no constraining force and the group will disintegrate. In our research we are concerned about the involvement group members have in upholding the norms of the group. "Upholding" the norms has six meanings: 1) following the norms oneself; 2) expecting others to follow them; 3) persuading others who are deviating from the norms to follow them; 4) reporting others who do not follow them; 5) accepting some responsibility for the consequences of others not following the norms; and 6) being willing to sanction deviance. The more group members are willing to undertake these actions in support of a norm, the more "collectivized" the norm becomes.

Table 1

PHASES OF COLLECTIVE NORMATIVE VALUE
AND SENSE OF COMMUNITY

Collective Normative Value	Community Value
A. *Proposing*	A. *Proposing*
0. No collective normative values.	0. No valuing of group as a community.
1. Individuals propose collective normative value.	1. Individuals propose that group be valued as a community.
2. Subgroup proposes collective normative value, partial acceptance of collective normative value.	2. Partial agreement that the group should be a community and proposal that it reach agreement on this.
B. *Expecting*	B. *Expecting*
3. Partial acceptance—partial expectation or call for expectation of the collective normative value.	3. Partial agreement that group should be a community, call for those who do not value the group as a community to value it.
4. Assumed general acceptance and expectation of the collective normative value.	4. Naive assertion that because the group is valued as a community it really is a community.
5. Disappointed expectation that people would uphold the collective normative value.	5. Disappointed expectation that the group really was a community.
6. Exhortation—assertion of expectation that collective normative value will be upheld in spite of deviance.	6. Reassertion of community value—in spite of difficulties building community.
C. *Enforcing*	C. *Collective Responsibility and Action*
7. Call for enforcement of the collective normative value.	7. Call for collective responsibility and community action to restore the community.
8. Expected enforcement of the collective normative value.	8. Expected collective responsibility and community action.
9. Full enforcement of the collective normative value.	9. Collective responsibility accepted and collective action undertaken to restore community.
D. *Compliance*	D. *Realized Community*
10. Complete compliance with collective normative value.	10. Full experience of group as community.

The Stage of the Collective Norm

While phases describe the relative strength of collective norms, they do not refer to their moral adequacy. In order to assess the moral adequacy of collective norms we have turned to Kohlberg's stage descriptions (Kohlberg, et. al., 1979). For the purposes of intervention and research, having a hierarchy of these stage-types is necessary because it provides us with standards for evaluating the moral adequacy of collective norms and values.

Our assessment of collective stages focuses primarily on those prescriptive statements made by individuals, acting as spokespersons for a group, upholding collective norms and values. As an illustration, I will quote from a Cluster student, Phyllis:

> "The point is that this school is supposed to be a community and in the community we are supposed to work for a common cause and we are supposed to be able to trust everyone else in the community."

We know from her Moral Judgment Interview, Phyllis' stage of moral reasoning about stealing is between Stages 3 and 4. In addition, we know from this statement that Phyllis perceived Cluster as having shared expectations for trust and cooperation. In trying to assess the stage of collective norm, we first observe that Phyllis is taking the perspective of the community and exhorting community members in the name of the community. In becoming a spokesperson for the community, Phyllis is not only describing what the norms and values of the community are but is also morally prescribing them on behalf of the community.

We maintain that it is reasonable to stage collective norms and elements for three reasons. First, all collective norms and elements originate with individual proposals and are "kept alive" for a group only through individuals interpreting their meaning when applying them in various situations. The process of developing collective norms and values is one in which an individual's prescriptive reasoning becomes the shared

prescriptive reasoning of a group. Second, moral stages provide us with a way of speaking about the relative "morality"
or "fairness" of certain collective norms and elements. Individuals can distinguish collective norms and values from their
own and evaluate the standards of the group against their
own standards. For example, individuals at higher stages with
a strong attachment to the group strive to influence their
group to the acceptance of more adequate moral norms.
Individuals at lower stages often do not understand or agree
with what they feel they are expected to do. Third, groups
appear limited in their abilities to arrive at certain decisions
and make certain policies. A collective stage concept may
help to explain certain group differences in a moral concern
and why a group can undertake a policy at one time in its
history that it could not have at another time.

The Community Element

The formation of collective norms requires a minimal sense
that members of a group value the group and are prepared to
cooperate in order to maintain or enhance it. In our research
we are primarily interested in references to community elements (justifications for norms which express a valuing of
the group as a community).

This involves valuing the solidarity, group consciousness,
and commitment to communal living which make up the
ideal of community. A community is a group in which there
is a radical commitment to sharing such that all the members
may, in the Biblical phrase, "live as one." Community exists
to the extent a group has developed such an expectation for
sharing and this expectation is fulfilled. In this respect, we
distinguish valuing the group as a *community* from valuing
the group as a pragmatic *organization*. For example, a school
may be valued as an organization for its personnel, facilities,
or academic program. These reasons are quite different from
valuing a school for the social qualities we have described as
constituting the essence of community. For a group to become a community, there must be a focus on the inner social

life of the group and a concerned effort to perfect that common life. The concept of "community" is, as Kantor (1972) says, a utopian ideal to which members of a group commit themselves voluntarily.

CONCLUSIONS

We are in the process of utilizing this conceptual framework and research methodology which I have outlined in longitudinal and cross-sectional studies. Longitudinal study involves determining what collective norms and elements have developed in a group and what progress and/or decline has occurred in terms of their stage and phase. Such information can help staff and students to reflect on their group's history and to set goals for the future. Cross-sectional study involves comparing schools with each other such that staff and students can become more aware of their relative strengths and weaknesses vis-a-vis similar schools. Because of the number of different factors which contribute to the development of a moral atmosphere, these comparisons can only be made with great caution. Our hope in conducting this research is that by becoming attentive to the moral atmosphere, educational practitioners can find ways of changing it in order to promote individual moral development and the realization of Dewey's proposal to build community in the school.

NOTES

1. In this chapter I will use the first person plural to refer to the work which I did in collaboration with Lawrence Kohlberg, Joseph Reimer, Ann Higgins, Marvin Berkowitz and Anat Abrahami, members of the Ford Project on the study of democratic high schools.

REFERENCES

Dewey, J. "My Pedagogic Creed." In M. Dworkin (Ed.), **Dewey and Education**. New York: Teachers College Press, 1959.

Kantor, E. **Commitment and Community: Communes and Utopias in Sociological Perspective**. Cambridge: Harvard University Press, 1972.

Kohlberg, L. "High School Democracy: Educating for a Just Society." In R. Mosher (Ed.), **Moral Education: A First Generation of Research and Development**. New York: Praeger (in press).

Kohlberg, L., Colby, A., Gibbs, J. Speicher-Dubin, B., Power, C., and Candee, D. **Assessing Moral Stages: A Manual**. Cambridge: Center for Moral Education, 1979.

Moos, R. H. **Evaluating Educational Environments**. San Francisco: Josey-Bass; 1979.

Power, C. "The Moral Atmosphere of the School: A Method for Analyzing Community Meetings." Unpublished qualifying paper, Harvard University, 1978.

Reimer, J. "A Study in the Moral Development of Kibbutz Adolescents." Unpublished doctoral dissertation, Harvard University, 1977.

Scharf, P. "Moral Atmosphere and Intervention in the Prison: The Creation of a Participatory Community in Prison." Unpublished doctoral dissertation, Harvard University, 1973.

Chapter 14

THE ORIGINAL SCHOOL BOARD POSITION IN THE EVALUATION OF MORAL EDUCATION PROGRAMS

Alan L. Lockwood

In this chapter I will first make some general comments about evaluation followed by a number of observations about research on moral education programs. Then I will suggest a general point of view—the original school board position—which I believe can help in generating an adequate and defensible approach to the evaluation of moral education.

THE AIM OF EVALUATION

The enterprise of evaluation is a complex one and can serve a variety of purposes. I am here concerned with the summative type of evaluation whose purpose is to determine the worth of a particular program; to answer the question: Is this program educationally worthwhile? In this context, an evaluation study is a type of research aimed at making a value judgment about a program. As such, summative evaluation studies can be distinguished from another type of research; that which tests hypotheses derived from theory with the aim of confirming, disconfirming, or revising theoretical claims.

Evaluation studies are of primary interest to persons in policy-making positions. Persons who must decide whether a particular program should be continued, discontinued, revised, or expanded. Policy-makers in funding agencies must decide how their monies will be spent. Policy-makers in schools must decide what shall be in their curriculum.

These two features of evaluation, its audience and its aim, suggest two bits of advice for persons interested in designing evaluation studies. First, studies should be designed and conducted with the cooperation of the relevant policy-making group. An evaluation study should be, in effect, the product of negotiation between program advocates and those who will make the final value judgment about the program. This negotiation helps assure that appropriate information will be collected. Second, evaluators must make explicit the criteria of educational value to be used in determining the educational worth of the program. I will return to these points later on.

I have suggested that evaluation research can be distinguished from research designed to test theoretical claims. Not only can such a distinction be made but, in practice, it should be made. I have found studies which apparently intended to test theoretical claims but whose focus wavered such that theory testing began to merge with program evaluation. The consequences of this are unfortunate as I will try to show in the following section.

CONFUSING THEORY-TESTING
WITH PROGRAM EVALUATION

A few years ago I completed a rather intensive review of research on the effects of moral development programs (Lockwood, 1978). A central purpose of most of the studies was to determine if a program based on Kohlberg's claims about moral development could significantly increase stage of moral reasoning as measured by the mean Moral Maturity Score (MMS). There was a general theoretical belief that student reasoning could be advanced by treatments emphasizing the discussion of moral dilemmas. Theoretically such discussions engendered cognitive conflict which required stage advance for resolution.

Most of these studies followed the tenets of conventional research design. That is, experimental and control groups were selected, pre- and post-tests of moral reasoning were administered, and statistical tests were performed to determine if the treatment groups made significant advances over the controls.

As I read the results of these studies I began to sense a curious pattern. When treatments failed to produce statistically significant advantages for the experimental groups the researchers seemed chagrined. Explanations of the findings had a tone of failure. On the other hand, when statistically significant advantages were found favoring the treatment groups, no such researcher disappointment was evident. At one level what I perceived as the researchers' feelings can easily be explained. After all, the researchers worked hard at setting up programs consistent with theoretical assumptions about moral development and, quite understandably, would be disappointed if their hard work could show no effect. There is, however, a deeper explanation to consider. I believe the aims of theory-testing became confounded with the aims of program evaluation such that the failure of a treatment to produce statistically significant effects was perceived as tantamount to showing the program was of no educational value.

When these studies are seen as program evaluations, two notable things occur. First, advance in mean Moral Maturity Score functions as the primary criterion of a program's educational value and, second, statistical significance becomes the equivalent of educational significance. From a program evaluation standpoint neither of these occurrences is desirable. I will comment here on statistical significance and later on the use of the mean Moral Maturity Score.

Statistical significance is substantially related to sample size. If, for example, we were conducting a one-tailed t-test on pre- and post-test mean Moral Maturity Scores for a single treatment group, using .05 as our level of statistical significance, the following would occur. A 40-point mean increase in MMS would not be significant with a sample of fewer than 14 subjects but would be with a sample of 14 or more. A 30-point mean increase in MMS would not be significant with a sample of fewer than 24 subjects but would be with a sample of 24 or more. A 15-point mean increase in MMS would not be significant with a sample of fewer than 83 subjects but would be with a sample of 83 or more. (These calculations assume a pre-post-test correlation of .40 and a standard deviation of 75.)[1] The point is, all things being equal, the larger the sample the smaller are the mean differences necessary for obtaining statistically significant differences.

If you are enamored of statistical significance you know what to do. With a large enough sample you can be virtually assured of attaining statistical significance with whatever change scores you obtain. Clearly, however, this begs the question of *educational significance*. How much change is enough to claim that something educationally worthwhile has happened to the students? I will claim later that we do not know enough about how to interpret change scores for them to be an adequate criterion of program effectiveness even when they are statistically significant.

So far I have stressed the role of evaluation in making a judgment of a program's educational worth and claimed we should not confuse theory-testing research with program evaluation. I've also claimed that we must be careful in interpreting tests of statistical significance. In formulating a sensible and defensible approach to program evaluation. however, we need more than a listing of do's and don'ts. We need a coherent general point of view from which we can generate and justify an approach to program evaluation. In the remainder of this chapter I will outline such a point of view and use it to set out an approach to evaluating moral education programs.

THE ORIGINAL SCHOOL BOARD POSITION

Evaluation studies are often used to make decisions about a program's continuance, modification, expansion, or elimination. Typically these decisions are made by a group responsible for the allocation of limited resources. That is, limits of time, money, human energy and ability do not permit schools to pursue all possible good ends. Choices must be made. By taking the perspective of members of such a group we can generate some useful ideas about evaluation.

In describing the group whose perspective we shall consider I will borrow without consent and with extraordinary looseness from John Rawls' notion of the original position (Rawls, 1971). Rawls was concerned with establishing principles of distributive justice for the regulation of social institutions. He argued that the justice of possible social arrangements could be assessed from an imaginative "original position" from which rationally self-interested persons unaware of what status they would hold in society, determine the fairness of various arrangements for the distribution of social goods. I am going to suggest, by loose analogy, an "original" school board position from which we can generate some defensible ideas about evaluation.

Consider the board as a group which must make decisions about the worth of educational programs for their school system. Also, assume the members are rational, accountable, open-minded, and well-intentioned—in addition, assume they do not all hold Ph.D.s in education.

By rational I mean they intend to make decisions supported by good reasons; not whim or expediency. By accountable I mean they must be able to explain and defend their decisions to a public constituency. By open-minded I mean they are not initially biased in favor or disfavor of any particular programs and will give all a fair hearing. By well-intentioned I mean they wish to do the best they can for the students and staff in their school system and are not seeking self-aggrandizement in some way. By limiting the presence of Ph.D's I mean they are not all fully aware of the theories behind particular programs nor are they trained in the intricacies of statistics and research design.

Rawls did not want us to think of his original position as an actual anthropological-historical event—a time when noble savages sat around a campfire discussing social philosophy. Similarly, I am not suggesting the original school board is an identifiable group currently, or ever, in existence. Its characteristics, (rationality, open-mindedness, etc.) are, however, those which many actual school boards would wish to claim for themselves. The original school board provides a scenario for thinking through evaluation ideas and forces program advocates to broaden their perspectives regarding what should be assessed in an evaluation.

With the original school board position in mind, imagine a scenario in which a program advocate and the board are meeting to design an evlauation study of a provisionally approved moral education program. Envisioning this as a dialectic process of role-taking, I believe that the following conclusions would be agreed upon:

Developmental Measures Should Not be the Major Determinant of a Program's Worth

Because the board is accountable and must be able to explain and defend the effects of a program to a general public, numerical development scores are of limited value. These scores indicate student progress toward a long-term goal but do not provide enough information about what happened to specific students in a particular program. This is partly because usefully detailed interpretations of change scores cannot be made precisely. For example, what can be said *qualitatively* about differences between two students, each with a 35-point increase, one of whom changed from 213-248 and another of whom changed from 241-276? The board's interest in students and its obligations of accountability require more information than can be obtained from any numerical measure of development.

The program advocate would also not want the program to be evaluated primarily on its ability to stimulate significant increases in developmental scores. There are two major reasons for this. One, from what is known about development, for any given period of time some students will be more "ready" to develop than others. As a result, during the time of program implementaion, some students would be measurably affected and others not. The advocate would not wish to use a measure which would show program effects for only some of the students. Second, there is more to development than stage advance. Current measures of development do not capture the breadth of student reasoning; what is often called "decalage." The advocate would want as complete a picture as possible of how student reasoning is affected by the program.

From the point of view of either a member of the board or of a program advocate it is inappropriate to rely on developmental measures as the sole or primary criterion of a program's effectiveness. Such measures should be part of a program's evaluation but not elevated to the major standard of educational value for a particular program.

Major Goals to be Assessed
Should be Distinctive to Moral Education

Recognizing the limitations of developmental measures for program evaluation, the advocate may be tempted to "tack on" measures of other educational outcomes which he or she believes the board will find appealing. For example, because the board is concerned with student welfare, a measure of self-esteem might seem appropriate or, because certain purposes of schooling appear unassailable, such as the teaching of reading and writing, assessment of these skills may seem advisable. Such measures can be useful in showing that a program does not have negative unintended effects but they should not be used as primary measures of program effectiveness. We can see why this is so if we take the school board point of view.

Members of the board oversee a variety of programs designed to pursue a variety of learning outcomes. Members of the board would not expect each program to pursue all possible desirable ends. The value of each program is determined by its ability to achieve its particular purposes. We would evaluate a science program on its ability to teach science; math on the ability to teach math, etc. Of course we would not want programs to have a deleterious effect on other school goals. For example, if a math program effectively taught math at the expense of student self-esteem, we would negatively evaluate the program. However, if the program had a positive effect on self-esteem but did not effectively teach math, we would still negatively evaluate it. The point is, a program must be evaluated on its ability to produce outcomes distinctive to its purposes, although we do not want it to impede student learning of other school goals.

Where does this leave the moral education advocate? Developmental measures are inadequate and measures of other school goals are useful only to show that the program does not do harm. What must be done, it seems to me, is to elaborate and specify aims of moral education which are distinct to its purposes and which go beyond stage advance. Simply put, the advocate must be able to show the program does things other school programs do not.

Within the limits of this chapter neither a full moral education program nor an evaluation study can be set out. I can, however, suggest roughly how the advocate might proceed in setting goals distinctive to moral education. For me, the distinctive general purpose of moral education is the enhancement of rationality in the ethical domain. At minimum, evaluation should focus on a program's ability to affect rationality in ethics.

Some evidence of increased rationality shows in changed moral perception, explication, and justification. For example:

> *Perception*: Does the program improve student ability to recognize moral issues, values, and points of view? Are students better able to identify conflicts of ethical values in public controversy, history, literature, community affairs, etc.? Can students more accurately and completely paraphrase the moral points of view of others? Can students better make important distinctions such as the difference between factual assertions and value assertions?

> *Explication*: Do students improve in their ability to express their own moral points of view clearly? Do students improve in their ability to focus on the moral points of view embedded in others' statements?

Justification: Do students increasingly go beyond simple value assertions to identify reasons why their assertions seem correct? Can students explain why they prefer some points of view over others? Do students' reasons become more complex and elaborate?

These categories and questions illustrate some student outcomes which could be assessed. It is intended that these outcomes be explicitly derived from a conception of rationality in the ethical domain. If measures of rationality such as cognitive complexity or critical thinking are employed they should involve ethical content. Assessment of general cognitive development, such as those based on Piaget problem-solving tasks provide a general assessment of reasoning ability but lack ethical content. Members of the board might feel that existing school programs adequately promote general cognitive development and that effects distinctive to the moral domain be demonstrated.

Teachers as Well as Students Must be Assessed

Members of the board have a well-intentioned interest in teachers as well as students. They realize that teachers must carry out approved programs and therefore their responses to the program must be assessed. At minimum, board members would be concerned with teachers' understanding of, commitment to, and administration of the program. For example:

Understanding: How do teachers articulate the purposes of the program? How do they explain the rationale for the program and its connection to the general aims of education? What criteria for program effectiveness do teachers subscribe to? To what extent do teachers' understandings correspond with the program's intent?

Commitment: To what extent do teachers believe the program is worthwhile? Do teachers feel the purposes and practices of the program should be a high priority for schooling? Do teachers find professional satisfaction in carrying out the program?

Administration: To what extent do teachers devise lessons consistent with program goals? Are class discussions and other activities conducted as intended by the program?

The program advocate would also be interested in such information partly because he or she would want to know if the program is implemented as intended and partly because such information can guide future modifications of the program or identify needed areas for in-service education. From both the advocates' and board's positions, assessment of teachers is needed for an adequate program evaluation.

Observational Data is Vital to Program Evaluation

The perspective on evaluation outlined so far shows the need for carefully collected observational data in program evaluation. Many of the questions of interest to the board and to the advocate require observational data. Such data can help judge the curriculum-in-practice and provide insight into possible unintended negative or positive outcomes of the program. It is impossible to develop here the variety of uses to which observational data can be put or the variety of questions which may guide its collection. At minimum, however, I think it is clear that the board must have a descriptive narrative so that they can explain to the public what is going on in the program and can document the evidence on which their final value judgment is made.

FINAL COMMENTS

This sketch of an approach to evaluation has used, as an example, a moral education program with the aim of promoting increased rationality in the moral domain. My intent has not been to advocate such a program but to show how the "original school board position" can help in developing a comprehensive and defensible approach to program evaluation. By taking seriously the interests of all those groups who have a part in judging these programs, it is to be hoped that the best interests of program advocates, students, teachers and the general public will be served.

NOTES

1. For a concise treatment of a variety of misuses of statistical significance, see, Bakan, D. "The Test of Significance in Psychological Research." *Psychological Bulletin*, 1966, 6, pp. 423-37.

REFERENCES

Lockwood, A. "The Effects of Values Clarification and Moral Development Curricula on School-Age Subjects: A Critical Review of Recent Research." *Review of Educational Research*, 1978, 3, pp. 325-64.

Rawls, J. A Theory of Justice. Harvard University Press, Cambridge, 1971.

Chapter 15

MORAL DEVELOPMENT
IN THE CONTEXT OF
BROAD EDUCATIONAL GOALS

Edwin Fenton

The topic of this chapter, "Moral Development in the Context of Broad Educational Goals," strikes me as particularly vital in the light of my experiences as the leader this fall of four twelve-hour workshops in civic or moral education. I have been flying general educational goals from my masthead whenever I do workshops in cognitive moral development. Not that I have rejected moral education. On the contrary, I believe in it so deeply that I take every opportunity to remind us that we have very little lead time for integrating our ideas into the mainstream of education in a democratic society. It's wonderful for us to get together for our favorite kind of shop talk, but belonging to this delightful club with its couple hundred select members, its exclusive Stage 3 handshake, and its in-group acronyms—MJT, DIT, SRM, and all that—may be an impediment to educational change, if we as club members fail to see our activities as integral parts of full educational programs in the schools.

We must examine the place of moral education programs within already existing school curricula and organizational patterns, but with all respect to Alan Lockwood, I do not think we can do so if we approach the problem from the original school board position, That position is an intriguing social science model useful for analysis and provocative of further thought, but it is in no way an accurate description of the educational world I live in.

Let me try my version of an empirical description to see if it fits your evidence. This description applies to present school board members, school administrators, caring teachers, parents, and students who want to get into selective colleges. The original school board members Lockwood described were rational, accountable, open-minded, and well-intentioned, and there were no Ph.D.s in education among them. There are a few doctorates among the real school administrators, but the "rational, accountable, openminded and well-intentioned" fall along a bell-shaped curve, rather than cluster near one pole. Moreover, most of them probably think at the conventional stage—three and four—rather than Stage 5, and they ask questions stemming from the social perspective those stages require.

If we intend to make a significant impact on the schools, we must answer the questions of teachers, parents, administrators, and school board members. We must answer them with data from careful observations, but important as our data may be, it is the appropriateness of our answers that will determine whether cognitive moral education, like so many other educational innovations, will become another meteor whose brief, flashy life soon fades in the great Beyond. Let me try to resurrect from memory the kind of questions I have been asked more than once this fall:

"If I spend a lot of time doing moral discussions, I can't cover the material, and college board scores will suffer, won't they?"

"The school board and the administration want us to stress basic skills. How can your program contribute to skills development? Or, at least, can you prove that it won't reduce the learning of skills?"

"What evidence do you have that moral education influences behavior? We need a program that can do something about vandalism and drugs. Is that what you do?"

"Does moral education have anything to do with turning kids on? My students are apathetic and unmotivated. Can you help?"

"Can you come back in a couple of months and give us some more help?"

Questions such as these reinforce other more basic questions, such as, "Does the program help with perceived school problems? Where does moral education fit in the ongoing school program? What is the reaction of the community? What does the program imply for staff development?"

To answer these questions, we need evaluation techniques directed to the perceived needs of our most vital clients—the teachers, administrators, board members, parents, and students. I think that we can gather that evidence through the use of what Feldmesser and Cline call triangulation—a combination of paper and pencil tests, interviews, and questionnaires directed to students, and observations. Without knowing that we were triangulating, my colleagues and I have been gathering data through these three techniques to assess progress in Carnegie Mellon's Civic Education Project which the Danforth Foundation has supported so generously for six years. But let me describe what we have been doing and what we have been able to find out by these techniques.

We began to organize Civic Education Units, usually consisting of fifty to sixty students, in September, 1975. They took social studies and English within the Civic Education framework five days a week and, in addition, they enrolled for two or three additional periods a week in a Community Activity Period focused on community building, the development of interpersonal skills, and a participatory governmental structure. Typically, students took part in about one more discussion a month in social studies, and a second moral discussion in literature. In addition, the governance structure involved discussion of real life civic and moral dilemmas.

The Project has broad educational goals, three of which are developmental. We stress personal development, focusing on self-knowledge, self esteem, and the development of a personal identity, one of the major tasks of adolescence. We try to facilitate cognitive development, in particular the development of formal operational thought. And, of course, we emphasize cognitive moral development. There are two additional but equally important goals: knowledge, and basic skills, particularly in reading, writing, speaking, and listening. Most educators find these broad goals adaptable to their school's goal statement. This educational fit helps teachers to understand that our Project is not just another add-on. Instead, it can become a vital part of a school's broad educational program.

We have evaluated the Project in three major ways. Since we had limited funds for evaluation and were functioning in typical schools, we were unable to establish control groups. This circumstance required us to use national norms where available for controls on standardized tests. We also used two types of measures for which controls were not so essential.

Two participant observers worked in project schools for a year. They were able to document that students' speaking skills, listening skills, ability to chair meetings and ability to work constructively in small groups increased significantly through this program of civic education. Observation told us how many students spoke under what conditions in response to what agendas, and with what clarity and force. These data have helped us to persuade educators in other school systems that cognitive moral education through a civic education project can contribute to basic skills.

We have also tried to make rough assessments of climate or atmosphere through interviews, and we now have about twenty hours of interviews with students in the Civic Education Project on tape. These tapes provide a wealth of anecdotal evidence and first-hand testimony that students find the civic education program far more attractive than the regular programs it replaced. Written questionnaires underline this conclusion. These data speak to motivation and attitude. And they persuade school people, even without statements about statistical significance.

Interviews also provide evidence that students who participate in this program think better of themselves than they did
before they enrolled. They say consistently that other people
respect them more, that their teachers treat them differently,
and that they think better of themselves. Evaluators ought to
empower practitioners to get at these vital matters by helping
them to develop good interview techniques, questionnaires,
plus paper and pencil tests, of which Rotter's test for internal
control is one good example.

We have used the STEP tests for social studies skills. They
provide statistically significant evidence that, compared to
national norms, students' social studies skills increased after
two years in our program. Students also achieved significant
gains on the Tests of Academic Progress-Composition, over
a two-year period, compared to national norms. Results such
as these assure school officials that a civic education program
based on developmental psychology can enhance the learning
of basic skills rather than result in their deterioration.

Results on six measures of citizenship have also been encouraging, although I report them with considerable mis-
givings since we did not have adequate control groups. We
selected sixty questions from among several hundred released
by the National Assessment of Educational Progress to measure six aspects of citizenship; knowledge of government and
its functions; values, particularly relating to racial and sexual
discrimination and prejudice; attempts to change school practices; attitudes toward politics; attitudes toward school and
instructional techniques; and teacher-student relationships.
We administered the instrument in May, 1979, to first- and
second-year students in the project and to classes of college-
bound students in the same grades in the school. (Many students enrolled in the Civic Education Project are not college-
bound.) We then compared the Civic Education group with
both the national norms and the non-Civic Education classes.
On each of the six measures, the experimental groups ex-
ceeded both the national norms and the non-Civic Education
classes. The results were particularly impressive in three areas:
attempts to change school, attitudes toward school and

instructional techniques, and teacher-student relationships. During the 1979-80 school year, we are administering two forms of this instrument as pre- and post-tests to experimental and control groups in seven schools in the project. By next June, we should have more reliable data to report.

Despite the fact that we did not have adequate controls to satisfy us from the perspective of the researcher, both school officials and parents find our data convincing and encouraging. It's the combination that counts—conventional goals such as more knowledge about politics and better attitude toward politics combined with more innovative outcomes, such as better attitudes toward school, and improved teacher-student relationships. People demand "both-and" from new programs; they are not satisfied with "either-or."

"So far, no moral education," I hear you thinking. We used the Moral Judgment Interview to assess moral development. On the whole, we found no change the first year, but statistically significant change in the second year. When I explain these findings to school board type people, I say that through a carefully organized program we are trying to get students to a stage at which they can understand the need for rules, articulate a sophisticated law and order position, and apply that thinking to new situations. I also explain that until they pass through such a stage, they cannot understand the deeper meaning of the Constitution, most of the world's great literature, and the Bible, or anything written by moral philosophers.

The intriguing evaluating instruments developed to assess moral judgment which were described in earlier chapters should make a valuable contribution to those of us who spend our lives in the schools. They promise to be relatively easy to administer and score, and not as expensive as some other instruments we have relied on. But we must remember to interpret them as Jim Rest suggested—half way, or two-thirds of the way to a someplace that people in the schools care about. And, we must be sharply aware of Marcia Mentkowski's researcher's fallacy—that instruments designed for research are the only appropriate ones with which to evaluate practice. X number of moral maturity points, significant or not depending on the size of the sample, often impresses only those people who hold doctorates, and not even the most sophisticated among these.

Lest I commit an interventionist's fallacy, let me amend my recommendations somewhat. Earlier in this chapter, I argued that educators demand "both-and" from new programs—both the best of conventional objectives and additional achievements. We shoud make similar demands of ourselves as evaluators. We should adhere to rigorous professional standards when we design an evaluation. And we should report our results both for other researchers and for the general public. In other words, we should make statements of statistical significance to one audience and report that we are twothirds of the way to where we want to get to another. We evaluators must seek the gift of tongues if we intend seriously to disseminate our secrets beyond the bounds of our exclusive club.

Chapter 16

MORAL EDUCATION:
LET'S OPEN THE LENS

Ralph L. Mosher

I hope to achieve two goals with these brief comments, to summarize some of what I have learned from a decade of applied work in developmental and moral education, and to argue that it is time to "mainstream" moral education in order to further our efforts for the all-around human development of students.

Frank Brown characterized the 1970's in American public education as a decade of the bland leading the bland. Au contraire for moral educators! For us it has been a time of particularly active field research and development. We have found that we can promote moral reasoning, and while the ability to think critically about right and wrong, about obligations and rights, is by no means all of morality, it is certainly an important part. There have been enough studies to persuade me that moral thought can be stimulated through curriculum and teaching: in American history, social studies, English, law, psychology and also in special curriculum modules of which Holocaust or Environmental Studies are examples. Furthermore we can show that children or adolescents who participate in classroom or school governance grow morally when they cooperate with other students in building social community within the school. Finally, in those rare instances where we have been able to "give away" knowledge about children's moral development to parents, the children were shown to benefit.

I do not think this consistent evidence of moral growth in response to education is a fluke. It has been found too many times in too many different groups of school children and in too many parts of the country to be explained away as a Hawthorne (or a Blatt) effect; to be attributed to scorer unreliability or to teaching to the Kohlberg test. It is no small accomplishment to be able to say in good conscience that we can promote moral reasoning in public schools without detriment to academic achievement. Indeed, this is probably the most important thing we have achieved as a movement in this decade.[1]

But there are major qualifiers to our claims for achievement. If there were not, we would either be very wise or out of business. The former is a much sought-after condition; in academia the second is worse only than a one-year non-renewable contract.

My first group of qualifers has to do with our capacity for documenting the changes effected by educational intervention: The average moral growth effected by "one-shot" courses of a semester's length or less is one-fourth or less of a Kohlberg stage for approximately half of the children who participate. A relatively small proportion of children in any school have been part of the experimental classes. Also, we have more data on gains in reasoning by adolescents than elementary school children. As yet insufficiently tested are the indications that the effects of systematic moral education may be greatest for younger children and for those children who are at a "natural" point of transition. Our evidence from longitudinal studies is skimpy, although it is encouraging. It suggests that a little bit of moral education can go a long way; once triggered, growth in moral reasoning may have considerable momentum.[2] But these are educated guesses in need of much careful study.

My second group of qualifiers takes note of the fact that the best moral discussion classes seem just about as effective as the best "Just Community" in promoting growth in moral reasoning. Thus, students in the Cambridge Cluster School averaged a gain of 1/4 of a moral stage per year. Some 40% of the students showed no growth or regressed; the principal movement was from Stage 2 to 3. No control data are available as to how much of this growth is natural and how much is the result of the school's programs. But the average development of Cluster School students was essentially equivalent to that of the best Stone Foundation moral discussion classes.[3] By "best" classroom moral education I mean the following: well-articulated moral dilemmas are discussed within existing or innovative subject matter; approximately 20 class periods are devoted to such discussions; the teacher is able to recognize moral stages in the students' talk and is effective in probing their thinking (e.g., asking "why?"); a cross-section of moral stages exists among the students. My experience is that educating teachers to provide such conditions for moral growth, while anything but simple, is more immediately practical and will require less absolute effort than to democratize classrooms and schools. However, we will need both forms of experience in any comprehensive moral education program.

Thirdly, there is considerable evidence that teachers haven't stayed with moral education programs. Kohlberg says that only one of 20 teachers in the Stone Foundation Study in the Boston area was still teaching moral dilemmas a year after the project ended.[4] He cites this as an example of a successful operation in which the patient died. Many of the first generation moral education projects have been similarly shortlived. In Brookline, which I know best, the attrition of active project teachers and counselors since 1973 has been heavy. Well over half of the original participating faculty are gone. In good part this has been because a number of the first generation have moved to major leadership roles elsewhere (e.g., Aubrey, Alexander, Dowd, Di Stefano, Paolitto and Sullivan at Brookline and Taylor and Wasserman at Cambridge). A hard core of deeply committed and productive teachers remain at both experimental schools but there has been significant staff turnover, and "burn-out" or cumulative fatigue because of unusual demands on the teachers' time and energy is a very real problem.

Lack of administrative support, which is a euphemism for tangible financial and moral backing by the superintendent, school board and principal, has played a role in the attrition of moral development programs. If teachers are to disseminate their curricula or train other teachers, there must be recognition and financial support for such activities. Large scale teacher training projects, such as those organized by Denton at Carnegie Mellon University, will surely contribute to the staying power of second generation programs in moral education. Also, it seems to me to be essential that moral education programs be "wholly owned" by the school systems in which they are to be implemented. In the meanwhile, the attrition facing moral education programs and their personnel, especially when the soft money runs out, is apparent as the solutions.

My fourth concern is that we have little evidence as to the practical consequences, in school or out of school, of the growth of children's moral reasoning as induced by education. One reason is that we have concentrated primarily on measuring increases in moral reasoning capacity. While increments, even small ones, in human thinking are unquestioningly important, we badly need to know what—if anything—goes with an average gain of one-fourth stage in moral reasoning. I do not wish to denigrate this kind of finding; many school enterprises that claim to be teaching kids to think flourish on much less evidence than this. But let me give you an example of outcomes of a different sort that have emerged from the study of the data on moral stage and school atmosphere.

Quite by chance from Travers' unrelated research,[5] I learned that S.W.S. students think more critically about their education and want to participate in formulating its conditions; are more concerned about local, state and federal government and participate far more extensively in political and social action in the community than do any other group of students at Brookline High School. And critical thinking about one's schooling and government plus political and social activism isn't attributable to academic track or socioeconomic status. There are many students at Brookline High School, as bright and as middle class, who do far less critical thinking about school and society and participation in them. What makes the difference is "S.W.S.," not "S.E.S." Assuming the moral stage growth found by Di Stefano in S.W.S. students is general, the Travers' data support Candee's argument that higher stages of development permit greater participation. They also provide evidence that participating in governing one's school and in building it as a small society can generalize to the larger community. And the converse of Candee's point is that such participation, in time, may affect the students' moral and social thought.

Masterson's data say that a student's stages of moral and ego development are related to behavior toward classmates and the teacher, and to who influences whom in classrooms.[6] For example, friendly Stage-3 kids are more likely to influence wary Stage-2 adolescents than are students at Stage 4 or teachers. Denton's data suggest that school grades improve in civic education programs. Admittedly, these are straws in the wind. Of one thing I'm sure, however. As we accumulate such evidence concerning the practical consequences of children's moral growth for them, the school or the home, our constituency will enlarge.

Let me now turn to some other research and development issues which face us in moral education. In commenting on what we've learned in a first generation of research I've already edged into these matters. Nor do I make any pretense of being exhaustive in what follows. But here are some of the research and development tasks which I see as needing attention:

A) What is a successful moral education program?

...Is it one which promotes normal development? ...accelerated development? ...one that prevents children from falling behind in moral understanding? ...Is it a program for children who elect it? ...should it be for all students? ...Is it an education in understanding the moral and social conventions of the family, church and state, in understanding why one should tell the truth, keep promises, care about others, act responsibly? ...or is such an education covert indoctrination? ...Is it an education which promotes autonomous moral thinking? ...principled thought? ...an education for moral action as well as judgment? ...and by what means? ...by classroom discussion, participation in social settings that are experienced as moral, by teacher advocacy like Durkheim's "priest of society?" ...by facilitation of democratic process in the classroom?

I am intentionally raising questions. My own abbreviated answer to these same questions is that a successful moral education program permits more growth, by any means other than indoctrination or punishment, thus promoting moral autonomy. To date, however, moral educators have tended to define success as anything which promotes slightly accelerated development in moral reasoning in one-half of the students in experimental classes. Clearly, our answers need to be more sophisticated than that.

B) A second issue confronting us is how to draw other curriculum areas in the secondary schools (for example, the sciences, mathematics, health, physical education, athletics) into moral education. Or is it vice versa? Morality is too important to be left to social studies teachers only! Current moral education projects are just beginning to seek this common cause.

Further, we need a major effort to involve elementary school teachers in moral education. My experience is that they are very much attuned to childrens' development and to education that will promote it. Morality obviously can't wait until high school. A few pioneering studies of how to promote administrators' moral thinking have been done. More need to be. Similarly, furthering teachers' own development as the aim of their professional education, which has been the focus of Sprinthall at Minnesota and Parsons at Utah, are promising innovations. Let me stress again, however, that so far no teacher training effort commensurate with the scope planned by Fenton for high school teachers is underway, or even talked about, for elementary schools.

Making childrens' moral development the responsibility of the school as a whole (and of the home and the church) is essential for several reasons. Primary among them is the evidence that moral growth seems to occur in small but progressive increments. No more than childrens' mental health can be left to school psychologists can morality be left to any one group of teachers (or, for that matter, to the schools alone). I have long argued that parents are the natural moral educators of their children. And I celebrate the appropriation of moral development theory and education by religious educators.

C. I am not talking, however, about a tower of Babel. How to create a coherent, progressive program of moral education for children, adolescents and young adults is a third issue. Class meetings to decide upon rules and discipline in Grade 5, discussion of the Holocaust in Grade 8, role-playing the constitutional debates in American history in Grade 11 and political action on behalf of local candidates for office in Grade 12 are not a coherent, systematic education for the moral choices facing young people. They are essentially ad hoc and determined more by who is interested in moral education than by any overall conception of moral growth or an education for it. Yet even these patchwork experiences are much more than we offer young people currently. Again, the point is that we need to coordinate curriculum, teaching and student participation in school governance with parent, family and religious education if we are to promote growth comprehensively.

D. Fourth, I feel strongly that we need to look for the effects of what we are doing on more aspects of the child's development than (gains in) moral reasoning. I am repeating this point intentionally. Is the child's behavior in class or out of it differen? How? Masterson, as noted, has found that one's stage of development does affect how one behaves toward both classmates and the teacher. Is the child's social behavior different? Travers' findings that educational and political thought as well as social and political participation are affected by democratic schooling have been mentioned already. They are as important a validation of the impact of the School-Within-A-School as are the gains in moral reasoning reported for these students by Di Stefano.[7] Does the adolescent's ego development, a broader strand of growth than any other, move in tandem with moral growth? The tentative answer seems to be yes, only more so.[8] Does the students' sense of competence grow in any way because of moral education or participation in school democracy? I have observed greater student self assurance in chairing meetings, in speaking publicly, in serving on committees to hire new faculty, in assuming leadership, in confronting faculty and peers on the part of many adolescents in the School-Within-A-School. But our singular pursuit of gains in moral reasoning at the .01 level or "the moral atmosphere" of the school have distracted us from many of the other effects we may, or may not, be having. It is time to open the lens through which we view and measure our world.

There is a converse. I first bumped into moral development as a by-product of teaching counseling to high school students. It was a serendipity. Only later did I understand how teaching empathy was related to morality. Gains in moral reasoning or development similarly may come where we least expect them or aren't trying for them. Social education, aesthetic education, drama, women's studies, etc. may all be carriers of unacknowledged effects of morality. Part of casting a wider net is to search out such effects. Taking an even wider view, I believe we ought to be as concerned to understand and educate for all around child development as for morality. To do so is a moral imperative for me as an educator. But in so doing we probably will promote character development, too. Growth seems as holistic as particularistic. Stimulation on one strand of the developmental helix (e.g., the self or ego) spills over onto another (morality) through interconnections we only partly understand.

My final point is really a summary statement. Personal growth happens in small, progressive steps. It does not take quantum leaps, even when we try very hard to make it do so. Piaget can relax about Americans' obsession with accelerating human development. They'll try, but they can't. What is feasible through education is to help people to actualize more of their personal potential and competence. If that is so, the task is to "give the psychology of moral development and education away" to as many teachers, administrators, parents and interested others as possible. That will begin to make morality a common cause rather than the special mandate or burden of moral educators. It is time, also, to recognize morality as but one competency among the many: rationality, social cooperation, love, which make our development as humans complete. The study of moral judgment needs to rejoin the larger body of the psychology of general human development. Similarly, it is time to "mainstream" moral education as one means to enhance overall human capability. This field has led a modest neoprogressivism in American public education. What we have learned can be very helpful in promoting other dimensions of human growth. If we are to avoid being the last hurrah for progressivism, then we need to turn our understanding and energy to collaborative endeavors to promore cognition, ego, affect, social competence, vocation, a sound body, the spiritual as well as character in all people. That is the ultimate meaning of a moral and a democrating education.

REFERENCES

1. Early studies of the powerful effect of moral education on children were done by M. Blatt, "Studies on the Effects of Classroom Discussions upon Children's Moral Development," doctoral dissertation, University of Chicago, 1970; P. Grimes, "Teaching Moral Reasoning to Eleven Year Olds and Their Mothers: A Means of Promoting Moral Development," doctoral dissertation, School of Education, Boston University, 1974; and L. Rundle, "The Stimulation of Moral Development in the Elementary School and the Cognitive Examination of Social Experience: A Fifth Grade Study," doctoral dissertation, School of Education, Boston University, 1977. Dowell's research with adolescents was similarly ground-breaking. See R. C. Dowell, "Adolescents as Peer Counselors: A Program for Psychological Growth," doctoral dissertation, Graduate School of Education, Harvard University, 1971.

2. See, for example, E. V. Sullivan and C. Beck, "Moral Education in a Canadian Setting." **Moral Education . . . It Comes with the Territory**, D. Purpel and K. Ryan, Eds. Berkeley: McCutchan Publishing, 1976, pp. 221-234; V. L. Erickson, "Deliberate Psychological Education for Women: From Iphiginia to Antigone," *Counselor Education and Supervision*, June, 1975, 14, pp. 297-309.

3. Personal communication with Professor Joseph Reimer of Boston University.

4. L. Kohlberg, "High School Democracy and Educating For a Just Society." **Moral Education: A First Generation of Research and Development**, R. Mosher, Ed. New York: Praeger, 1980.

5. Personal communication with Professor Eva Travers of Swarthmore College.

6. M. C. Masterson, "Structures of Thought and Patterns of Social Behavior: Stage of Ego and Moral Development and Their Relationship to Interpersonal Behavior," doctoral dissertation, School of Education, Boston University, 1979.

7. A. Di Stefano, "Adolescent Moral Reasoning After a Curriculum in Sexual and Interpersonal Dilemmas," doctoral dissertation, School of Education, Boston University, 1977.

8. See P. Sullivan, "A Curriculum for Stimulating Moral Reasoning and Ego Development in Adolescents," doctoral dissertation, School of Education, Boston University, 1975; V. L. Erickson, "Deliberate Psychological Education for Women;" N. A. Sprinthall, "Learning Psychology by Doing Psychology: A High School Curriculum in the Psychology of Counseling." **Developmental Education**, G. D. Miller, Ed. St. Paul: Minnesota Department of Education, 1976, pp. 23-43.

CONTRIBUTORS

James R. Bode is Associate Professor of Philosophy at the Ohio State University-Lima. He has served as consultant to the National Endowment for the Humanities and has published articles in developmental ethics, logic and epistemology.

James L. Carroll is Assistant Professor of Educational Psychology at Arizona State University. He is involved in helping school psychologists develop intervention and evaluation skills. His recent articles have appeared in *Professional Psychology* and *The Journal of School Psychology.*

Anne Colby is a lecturer and Research Associate at the Graduate School of Education, Harvard University. She has been a member of the editorial board for the *Journal of Moral Education*, and has contributed to numerous journals. She is currently completing the Standard Form Moral Judgment Scoring Manual, and is applying developmental perspectives to clinical and counseling psychology.

V. Lois Erickson is Associate Professor of Educational Psychology at the University of Minnesota. Her many publications are in the areas of developmental counseling psychology, teacher education, and adult development. She received the 1976 American Personnel and Guidance Research Award for an article presenting a progress review of her longitudinal study of the ego and moral development of the sample of young women on which this article is based.

Edwin Fenton is Professor of Education at Carnegie Mellon University and Director of its Education Center. He is the author or editor of approximately fifty books and texts in history and civic education, and one of the leaders and spokespersons for moral education. His most recent venture is the development of a National Leadership Training Program for Leading Civic and Moral Discussions.

John C. Gibbs is Assistant Professor of Developmental Psychology at Ohio State University. His articles on sociomoral development and on psychological research have appeared in the *Harvard Educational Review, Human Development*, and *American Psychologist*. He is also interested in the developmental assessment of modes of dyadic conflict resolution.

Louis A. Iozzi is a member of the faculty in the Department of Education, Cook College, Rutgers University and its Director for the Institute for Science, Technology and Social Science Education. The Institute has developed an extensive curriculum project called "Preparing for Tomorrow's World."

Lawrence Kohlberg is Professor at Harvard University's Graduate School of Education and Director of its Center for Moral Education. He has developed and validated a Moral Judgment Instrument that is the definitive instrument for measuring sequential stage development. He is the author or co-author of countless articles, chapters and monographs, among the most popular are, "The Cognitive Developmental Approach to Socialization," in D. A. Goslin (Ed.), **Handbook of Socialization Theory and Research**; "A Modern Statement of the Platonic View," in Sizer (Ed.), **Moral Education**; "From Is to Ought: How to Commit the Naturalistic Fallacy and Get Away With It," in Mischel (Ed.), **Genetic Epistemology**; and "Moral Stages and Moralization: The Cognitive-Developmental Approach," in T. Lickona (Ed.), **Moral Development and Behavior: Theory, Research and Social Issues.**

Lisa Kuhmerker is Director of the Hunter College Program for Gifted Youth, and Associate Professor in the Department of Curriculum and Teaching. She is the founder and editor of the *Moral Education Forum*, and was a founding member and the first president of the Association for Moral Education. She is an active speaker and writer in the U.S. and has also lectured on moral education in Germany, Holland, Belgium, England, Italy and India.

Marcus Lieberman is Assistant Professor of Education at the Harvard Graduate School of Education. He teaches courses in statistics, research methodology and evaluation. He also conducts research on appropriate empirical techniques for analyzing data from cognitive-developmental studies and related educational applications.

Alan Lockwood is Professor of Curriculum and Instruction at the University of Wisconsin-Madison. He received his doctorate at the Harvard Graduate School of Education. His major scholarly interests lie in the field of value education; recent publications have considered the right to privacy as it is affected by values education programs and what research has shown about the effects of vaues education programs.

Marcia Mutterer Mentkowski is Director of Evaluation and Associate Professor of Psychology at Alverno College. She is an author of **Valuing at Alverno: The Valuing Process in Liberal Education**, and principal investigator of an NIE grant to validate the Alverno curriculum. She has been a visiting scholar at the Center for Moral Education at Harvard, developed curriculum in moral education for students from elementary school through college as well as for teachers and law students.

Ralph L. Mosher is Professor of Education at Boston University, former Chairman of the Department of Counseling Psychology and Director of Programs in Human Development and Education. He has been a consultant to the School-Within-A-School in Brookline, Massachusetts for the past five years and has been a consultant for many other school programs with a moral education dimension.

Edward A. Nelsen is Associate Professor of Educational Psychology and Associate Director of the I. D. Payne Laboratory at Arizona State University. He has published research concerning honesty in *Developmental Education* and *Multivariate Behavioral Research*.

Roger A. Page is Assistant Professor of Psychology at the Ohio State University-Lima. He is engaged in research on assessing the development of moral/ethical reasoning and the effects of moral education strategies. A recent publication is "Longitudinal Evidence for the Sequentiality of Kohlberg's Stages of Moral Judgment in Adolescent Males," *Journal of Genetic Psychology.*

June Paradise-Maul is a Management Training Executive with A. T. & T. Long Lines Training Organization. She has been a Visiting Scholar at the Center for Moral Education and an Assistant Professor at Rutgers University's Center for Coastal and Environmental Studies, working on courses addressing themselves to ethical issues at the interface of science, technology and education.

Clark Power is a Research Associate at the Center for Moral Education at Harvard University's Graduate School of Education. For the past four years he has participated in a Ford Foundation Study of democratic alternative high schools and is preparing the results of this research for publication.

James R. Rest is Professor of Educational Psychology at the University of Minnesota. Ten years ago he was at Harvard's Center for Moral Education where work was begun on objective tests of moral judgment. His research has been primarily devoted to developing the Defining Issues Test and has culminated in the text **Development in Judging Moral Issues,** which explores the nature of moral judgment and its evaluation.

John M. Whiteley is Vice Chancellor-Student Affairs and Professor of Social Ecology at the University of California, Irvine. He was elected Fellow of the American Psychological Association in 1978. He is the Founding Editor of *The Counseling Psychologist*, of the Division of Counseling Psychology of APA. In addition, he is also the producer of over 100 educational and psychological films.

2

Keith Widaman is a graduate student at the Ohio State University, writing his doctoral dissertation on the relation between differential and experimental approaches to the measurement of ability. Other professional interests are in socio-moral development, cognitive development and developmental methodology.

APPENDIX

Sources for Evaluation Instruments
(Listed in Alphabetical order)

Defining Issues Test: Write to Professor James R. Rest, University of Minnesota, 330 Burton Hall, Minneapolis, MN 55455, enclosing your research proposal. Highly recommended: **Development in Judging Moral Issues**, by James R. Rest, University of Minnesota Press, 1979.

Environmental Issues Test: Write to Professor Louis A. Iozzi, Director, The Institute for Science, Technology, Social Science Education, Rutgers, The State University, Doolittle Hall, New Brunswick, NJ 08903.

Ethical Reasoning Inventory: Write to Professor James Bode, Department of Philosophy, or Professor Roger Page, Department of Psychology, both at Ohio State University, 4240 Campus Drive, Lima, OH 45804. (Enclose copy of research proposal, and $7.50 for permission for use.)

Moral Atmosphere Interview Scoring: Contact Clark Power or Anne Higgins at the Center for Moral Education, Harvard University Graduate School of Education, Larsen Hall, Appian Way, Cambridge, MA 02138, Tel. (617) 495-3546. A manual for scoring is in preparation and requires training at the Center for its use.

Moral Judgment Instrument: Standard Scoring: Contact the Center for Moral Education, Harvard University Graduate School of Education, Larsen Hall, Appian Way, Cambridge, MA 02138, Tel. (617) 495-3546. The MJI is available in Forms A & B, both forms scored by the Standard Scoring Manual ($20.00). Annual Summer Scoring Workshops are scheduled. A set of cases is available for prospective scorers to test if their reliability meets acceptable standards. Scoring services are available at approximately $10.00 per protocol, with exact fees depending on the size and the nature of the project.

Socio-Moral Reflection Measure: Write to Professor John Gibbs, Ohio State University, 1945 High Street, Columbus, OH 43219.

Sources for Other Measures Listed in the Text

Loevinger Measures of Ego Development, including the Sentence Completion Test: published in Loevinger, J. & Wessler, R. **Measuring Ego Development**, Vol. 1. San Francisco: Jossey, Bass, 1970. Write to Professor Loevinger at Washington University in St. Louis, MO 63130.

Adaptive Style Inventory: Write to Professor David Kolb, Department of Organizational Behavior, Case/Western Reserve University.

The College Self-Expression Scale: "A Measure of Assertiveness," *Behavior Therapy*, 1974, 5, 165-71.

Measure of Vocational and Personal Issues: Write to Professor L. Knefelkamp, College of Education, University of Maryland.

Test of Cognitive Development: Write to Professor J. Renner, School of Education, University of Oklahoma.

Available from McBer & Company, 137 Newbury Street, Boston, MA 02116:

> **Analysis of Argument**
> **Learning Style Inventory**
> **Life History Excercise**
> **Picture Story Excercise**
> **Test of Mathematical Analysis**

Available from Harcourt, Brace & World, New York, NY:

> **Watson-Glazer Test of Critical Thinking**